Basic plant care involves choosing the right location.
Before you buy a plant of your choosing, make sure you
have an appropriate place for it in your home.

BRIGHT LOCATION

Location:
— bright (at least 2000 lux)
— warm or cool
— dry or humid air

What's a good place for it?
— in windows facing east or west
— in places where the sun shines into
the room for several hours
— three to five feet from a large window
that faces south or southwest
— in bright apartments with light walls and
floors and large windows with no curtains

Plants that like bright locations:
Pages 86–103
At a glance: page 160

PARTIAL SHADE

Location:
— partial shade (1000–2000 lux)
— warm or cool
— dry or humid air

What's a good location for it?
— where the sun shines into the room
for only a few hours
— three to five feet from a large window that
faces south or southwest
— in places exposed to indirect light (such as beside or under windows)
— in or right next to windows

Plants that like partial shade:
Pages 104–111
At a glance: page 160

ANJA FLEHMIG

Indoor Plants for Beginners

▶ Plant Care Basics
▶ Choosing Houseplants
▶ Suggested Plants for Every Location

More Than 290 Color Photos
by Friedrich Strauss

Illustrations by Renate Holzner

BARRON'S

6

Contents

Plant Arrangements

Plant Care

Plant Care

he Right Environment

Basic care for plants from foreign lands involves finding the right place for them in our homes.

Of course, good, loving care that involves regular watering, feeding, and transplanting is important. But if the plants aren't placed in the right location, all our other efforts may be in vain.

Habitat Factors
In the wild, the appearance and propagation of plants are strongly influenced by external conditions in their immediate surroundings; these include
▶ Soil quality (important as source of nutrients and water supply)
▶ Temperature (influences speed of metabolic processes)
▶ Light intensity (source of energy for photosynthesis)
▶ Amount of precipitation (important for transpiration, which is the motor that drives the movement of substances within the plant)
▶ General climatic conditions such as length of day, temperatures during day and night, and the changes from winter to summer.

This adaptation to natural habitat has been perfected through evolution to the extent that it's very stressful for plants to be moved from their home environment to a different climatic range.

Adjustment to Living Indoors
Growing and cultivating plants involves using a greenhouse to help the transplants from foreign countries adapt as well as possible to our local climate with reduced light intensity and a long, relatively dark winter season. Then the plants still have to make the change from the optimized conditions of the greenhouse to those of the home. It's a good idea for inexperienced houseplant gardeners to start with robust strains so that they don't lose their enthusiasm for their new hobby. Here's a tip:
▶ Plants with dark green, firm, somewhat leathery leaves are less sensitive to shortcomings in environment and care than are plants with light green or variegated, thin, and filigreed leaves.

Most palms thrive indoors only in warm, sunny places.

Choosing the Right Spot in Your Home

Light is a crucial factor for plant growth. Light conditions indoors are greatly reduced in comparison with outdoors; light reaches the plants only indirectly, through panes of glass of different sizes, and it is often reduced by surrounding buildings and trees. Even in a large south-facing window, light intensity in full sunshine right behind the glass reaches only around 5000 lux, whereas in nature, depending on the time of day, it may reach between 20,000 and 100,000 lux.

There are four categories of houseplants:
▶ Plants that like sunny locations (light intensity of 3000–5000 lux)
▶ Plants that like bright locations without direct exposure to the sun (light intensity of at least 2000 lux)
▶ Plants that thrive in partial shade (light intensity between 1000 and 2000 lux)
▶ Plants that get by with very little light and that thrive in shaded locations (but at light intensities in either case not much below 1000 lux)

Measuring Light Intensity

Light intensity can be measured with a lux meter (available in specialty shops). But even the plants will tell you if they like their location. There's rarely a problem with a location that's too sunny, but with dark locations some typical signs of light deprivation will show up after a few days:
▶ The plants stop growing
▶ The leaves turn yellow and fall off
▶ New shoots reach out and grow toward the light
▶ Variegated leafy plants lose their coloration and turn a homogenous green, and
▶ Blooming plants either drop their buds or fail to grow any

What to Do in Case of Excess Light

Sunny locations—especially at midday in the summer months—must be shaded to keep leaves from becoming burned. Heat buildup must be avoided through appropriate means such as shading and ventilating.

Plants for Warm, Humid Climes
Well-lighted bathrooms are the ideal place for indoor bamboo and ferns.

What to Do in Case of Light Deficiency

Darker locations can be artificially illuminated with growing lights. For supplemental light in the winter, these lights should be turned on for four to six hours; if they are the only source of light, they should be left on for about twelve hours a day. Normal incandescent lights, halogen, and fluorescent bulbs are not an adequate substitute for sunlight. Specialty shops offer a broad selection of special plant lights.

Warm or Cool?

Just as plants have different requirements for light, they react differently to temperature. Depending on where the plants originate, they require a warm or a cool location. It's usual to distinguish between
▶ warm (above 70°F/22°C)
▶ tepid or moderately warm (61–65°F/16–18°C, often with overnight decline of 37–39°F/3–4°C)
▶ cool (41–54°F/5–12°C, outdoors in the summer)

Higher temperatures accelerate growth, and that requires energy. With the help of light, energy is built up, so it's generally true that the warmer the location, the brighter it can be; the cooler, the darker it can be.

The temperature of the soil also plays an important role in how plants

The kitchen window is an appropriate location for various herbs and blooming potted plants.

thrive, since it has a direct effect on how the roots grow.

Polystyrene or cork under the flowerpots prevents cooling of the root balls on cool windowsills; similarly, this insulating measure also guards against overheating on windowsills that are directly above a heating element.

Humidity

The warmer a room is, the lower its humidity, especially in winter when the central heating is in full operation and there's not much ventilation.

▶ Warm and dry locations (approx. 30–40 percent humidity) are especially well suited to cactuses and succulents as well as to plants that have coarse, leathery leaves.

▶ Warm, humid locations (around 60 percent humidity) are appropriate for leafy plants with large, soft leaves, ferns, and orchids. But excess humidity may encourage growth of fungi.

▶ Most plants won't thrive in cool, humid locations (around 60 percent humidity), and they may become subject to fungal infestations.

CROSS REFERENCE
Increasing Humidity,
page 23

Guests from Foreign Lands

Overview

Caring for Tropical Rain Forest Plants

warm the entire year
high humidity
bright to partially shaded
location sheltered from draft
avoid watering epiphytes too
frequently; better to mist them

Caring for Tropical Mountain Forest Plants

temperate (57–65°F/14–18°C)
high humidity
bright to partially shaded
location

Caring for Desert Plants

warm the entire year
reduced humidity
sunny location
water sparingly; don't mist
maintain rest periods

Caring for Mediterranean Plants

in summertime, sunny and
sheltered from rain outdoors
in the winter, protected from
frost; bright and cool indoors

Tropical Rain Forests

In tropical rain forests, the temperatures year-round remains between 75 and 86°F /24 and 30°C, and humidity is nearly 90 percent. The length of the days is always the same with about twelve hours each of daylight and darkness. Philodendron, Split Leaf Philodendron, varieties of Ficus, Maranta (prayer plant), and orchids are some of the plants that come from the tropical rain forests of Africa, Brazil, Indonesia, and the Philippines.

Tropical Mountain Forests

The climate in the mountainous regions of the tropics is characterized by rainfall, fog, and cool temperatures.

The moist, cool mountain forests of Borneo, Ecuador, New Guinea, Peru, Sumatra, and Venezuela are home to numerous ferns and the wild forms of the Kalanchoe hybrids.

If you are familiar with the climatic conditions in which our houseplants normally grow, it's much easier to understand the care they need.

Tropical Savannas

The farther we go from the equator, the less precipitation there is. In the savanna regions of the earth the daytime temperatures are still high, but precipitation falls only at certain times of the year, so vegetation is forced to deal with fairly long periods of drought.

Amaryllis, Poinsettia, and palms are some of the plants that grow in the savanna regions of Argentina, Australia, Brazil, Colombia, Venezuela, central Africa, and central Madagascar.

Desert Regions

In places where precipitation levels are even lower, semi-arid regions gradually give way to deserts, with hot daytime temperatures, frost at night, and abundant sunshine.

Plants such as Aloe, Ponytail Palm, Jade Plant, Madagascar Palm, Living Stones, and Yucca come from the desert areas of Australia, India, Madagascar, North and South Africa, the southwestern United States, and the southern part of South America.

Mediterranean Region

In the Mediterranean region, the natural habitat of such plants as Bougainvillea, Common Fig, and Canary Island Date Palms, there are warm to hot, dry summers and fairly rainy, warm winters with no frost. The change between seasons is also noticeable through marked changes in the length of the days.

Cape Flora

The southern tip of Africa, with its hot summers and warm, humid winters is home to Calla Lilies, Lindens, Clivia, and the *Pelargonium* genus.

CROSS REFERENCE
Container Plants for Winter Gardens pages 80–81

Identifying Suitable Locations

Overview

In a Sunny, Bright, and Large Window

Weeping Fig or Rubber Tree, Fiddle Leaf Fig, Kentia Palm, Columnea, Yucca

In a Bright, Small Window

Alocasia, Caladium, Dragon Plant, Fishtail Palm, Fiddle Leaf Fig, Coconut Palm, Stephanotis, Croton, King Sago Palm, Screw Pine, Sword Fern

Partial Shade Away from a Window

Parlor Palm, Clivia, Dieffenbachia, Split Leaf Philodendron, Flamingo Flower, Rubber Tree, Syngonium, Schefflera, short-lived flowering plants

Shady Corners, Dark Corridors

Drocaena marginata, ivy, Spathiphyllum, Spider Plant, Climbing Philodendron, Fatsia Japonica (Fatsia or Japanese Aralia)

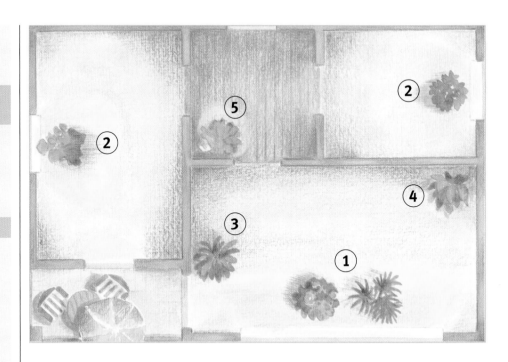

Different Amounts of Light

The illustration above shows how light can vary in intensity and angle in different rooms.

It's obvious that the light depends heavily on the size and orientation of the windows: rooms that face south and west let more light into the room than ones that face east and north.

The larger the window, the more light is available. It's important to note that the light comes from just one side.

1 Sunny, bright location in a large south-facing window

2 Bright location in a fairly small window that faces west or east

3 Partially shaded location three to six feet from a large south-facing window

4 Shaded location in the corner of a room about ten feet from a large south-facing window

5 Shaded location in the corner of a room that has a small north-facing window. Plants in these locations need eight to twelve hours of additional light per day from a growing light.

CROSS REFERENCE
A Place in the Sun, page 138
Greening Up Shaded Spots, page 142

CROSS REFERENCE
Life-Giving Light, pages 12–13
Problem Solving, page 136

Each room offers different conditions.
The better we are at recognizing them, the better we can accommodate our plants.

Bedroom: Bright and Cool

A cool, bright bedroom with temperatures between 60 and 68°F/16 and 20°C is an ideal spot for some types of plants, such as Cyclamen, Azalea, Winecup Primrose, Spider Plant, and Indoor Linden. It's also a good place for plants that need a rest period in the autumn and winter, such as Amaryllis, Clivia, Bougainvillea, and Passion Flower.

Remember that plants need considerably less water in cool places; water them only when the root balls are dry on the top surface.

Hallway: Dark and Drafty

Usually hallways are not very bright; they tend to be cool and drafty because of opening and shutting doors. But there are still a number of houseplants for inhospitable rooms that can make an entryway seem more friendly.

Cast Iron Plant and Ivy can get by with very little light and are also very robust.

In extreme cases a growing light can be used. To provide color, add some short-lived potted plants that can be easily replaced.

Bathroom: Warm and Humid

The bathroom is continually gaining acceptance as a "living" room for plants because it is warm and comfortable. Plants that come from tropical forests and that don't need too much light thrive in the moist and warm conditions; these include grasses, many types of palms, ferns, and bromeliads. Because bathrooms often don't have many surfaces for holding plants, the best choices for plants are often small, erect ones or hanging ferns and similar plants.

CROSS REFERENCE
Thumb Test, page 22

CROSS REFERENCE
Adding Greenery to Staircases and Hallways, page 136

Watering

**Most houseplants don't dry out;
rather, they are subjected to excessive
or improper watering.**

When a plant's leaves hang down, it's not necessarily a sign that it needs to be watered. Quite the contrary: there is too much water in the top of the pot and the root ball is sopping wet.

Plants with Varying Thirst

Many plants will tell you by the way they grow, the size of their leaves, and the shape of their leaves whether they need a little water or a lot.

▶ Large, solitary plants with big leaves (such as Ornamental Banana), plants with large, soft leaves (such as Indoor Linden), Mediterranean container plants (such as Common Fig), and plants that come from tropical marshy areas (such as Umbrella Plant) need lots of humidity, since lots of water evaporates through their large leaf mass.

▶ Smaller plants (such as Maidenhair Fern and Dwarf Pepper), plants with a comparatively smaller leaf mass (such as Sansevieria), plants with leathery, coarse leaves (such as rubber trees and Sansevieria), cactuses, and succulent plants with fleshy leaves or stems that store water (such as Jade Plant and Flaming Katy, and Ponytail Palm, respectively) usually get by with less humidity.

Further Considerations

Location and type of pot also play a significant role in a plant's water usage.

▶ In general, it's safe to conclude that plants that are placed in a warm, bright location need more moisture than plants that are kept in a darker and cooler spot.

▶ Plants in a large container need more water than plants in small pots, since more water evaporates from a large surface area than from a small one.

▶ Plants in clay pots and unglazed terra-cotta vessels need to be watered more frequently than plants in plastic, glazed clay, or metal pots, since more water evaporates through the pores of the clay or terra-cotta.

Green and white elegance for a bright location: Orchids, Flowering Begonias, Ivy, Wax Plant, Spathiphyllum, and African Violet.

Water, Elixir of Life

Just like light, water is vitally important to all living things. With plants, it fulfills several tasks:
▶ It aids in absorption of nutrients from the soil (exchange of water ions at the roots for the necessary nutrient ions).
▶ It serves as a medium for transportation within the plant; there is a steady stream of water in special vessels, which serve mainly to convey nutrients to the various organs.
▶ It is the basis of the suction that extends from the roots to the leaves. When the plant gives up water by transpiration through the leaves, that creates a suction in the small canals that extends down to the tiniest root tips. This suction helps transport nutrients from the roots to the leaves.
▶ Transpiration also serves as a protection against overheating, for the water that evaporates through the openings in the leaves humidifies and cools the surroundings.
▶ It is an essential component of individual plant cells and contributes to their stability.

Hard or Soft Water?
The composition of tap water is different from place to place. Water hardness, or its lime content, is a significant factor in water used for plants. (Water hardness is rated on a scale that measures mg/L of $CaCO_3$, and can be determined by contacting the personnel at your local water supply facility.)
▶ Soft water contains up to 75 mg/L of $CaCO_3$. One sign of particularly soft water is when soap creates lots of suds and is difficult to wash off.
▶ Moderately hard water falls in the range of 75 to 150 mg/L. This water seems "normal" and is fine for most houseplants. Still, it's better if the water for plants is not used straight from the tap, but is left to stand overnight (or for a couple of days) in the watering can.
▶ Hard water contains more than 150 mg/L of $CaCO_3$.

Watering Bromeliads
Bromeliads are the only plants that should be watered in the funnel of the leaves.

Infallible signs of hard water are lime deposits in pots or electric heaters, on fixtures, and in the bathtub.

Generally speaking, hard water is not good for houseplants, and it should not be used for misting.

Hard water can be "softened" by using an ion exchanger or chemicals (see page 27). People who want to be a little more conscientious can boil the water so that part of the lime precipitates as scale.
▶ Distilled water is not suitable for watering, since it lacks the necessary minerals.
▶ Rainwater is not always recommended for watering houseplants, since it is often contaminated by pollutants in the air.

Basic Watering Rules
▶ Use water at room temperature (approximately 68°F/20°C) for watering houseplants.
▶ It's a good idea to let water stand overnight.
▶ It's preferable to water plants in the morning so that excess water can be poured out in the course of the day.
▶ It's better to water thoroughly and then let the root ball dry out than to water just a little each day.

Just as houseplants are all different from one another, they all have different needs for water and ways of watering.

▶ Use only softened water for plants that are sensitive to the cold.

Water from the Air: Misting
Moisture content in the air plays a particularly important role in the life of houseplants that come from warm, humid, tropical, and subtropical regions.

The highest atmospheric humidity in the house (at high temperatures) is in the bathroom. But that may not be bright enough for tropical plants, or there may not be enough good surfaces on which to put plants. The humidity in other rooms can be increased in several ways:
▶ Mist the plants at least once a day with room-temperature, lime-free water.
▶ Place several large-leafed plants together so that each one benefits when the others are misted.
▶ Place the plants on a dish filled with gravel and water.
▶ Put the flowerpot inside a second, somewhat larger pot; fill the space with vermiculite or gravel and keep it as moist as possible.
▶ Keep plants that need lots of humidity in a greenhouse, a cold frame, or an enclosed flower box where the humidity can be kept constant.

When, How, and How Often to Water

Overview

What's the best time of day to water?

Usually in the morning, in the summer in sunny locations; with especially thirsty plants, both morning and evening; never water in strong, direct sunlight.

When should a plant be watered?

When the surface of the soil feels dry; when the flowerpot seems especially light.

When is immersion appropriate?

When plants are particularly dried out, i.e., when water immediately runs out of the drain hole or doesn't get into the root ball.

Where should a plant be watered?

It's best to water directly onto the root ball or into the saucer under the plant.

Thumb Test

You can't go wrong if you use your thumb or index finger to test the moisture of the top layer of soil in the pot before watering. If the surface feels dry and crumbly, the plant needs more water. If it's moist and bits of soil stick to your finger, you can wait a while before watering.

Water from Above

Most houseplants can simply be watered from above, and directly onto the root ball rather than onto the leaves. Give the plant enough water so that the surface of the soil is good and damp and a little water collects in the saucer beneath it. Excess water that hasn't been absorbed after an hour or two can be poured off to avoid waterlogging.

Unfortunately, there is no general schedule for watering houseplants. The quantity of water is dictated by the type of plant, its phase of growth, its location, and the size of the pot.

Watering from Below

With plants that have hairy, velvety, fleshy, or soft leaves (such as African Violet and Soleirolia), or that provide ground cover (such as Creeping Fig), it's best to add water to the coaster beneath the pot; that way the leaves stay dry and don't rot. The plants suck the water up quickly, so here, too, excess water can be poured off after a couple of hours.

Increasing Humidity

It's a good idea to mist plants that have a pronounced need for humidity once or twice a day with lime-free water at room temperature, and to keep the plants on a thick drainage layer of gravel, clay, or pumice. The coaster should be filled with just enough water so that the upper half of the stones and the pot itself remain dry. Humidity in the immediate vicinity of the plant increases through evaporation of the water on the large surface area of the stones.

Immersion Bath

Ferns, Orchids, Azaleas, plants with hirsute leaves, and even Cactuses will appreciate an occasional immersion bath during their main growth period in the spring and summer. Place the pot up to its upper rim in a large container filled with water at room temperature until air bubbles cease to rise; at that point the root ball has drunk its fill. Immersion baths are also the right choice for hanging plants that may not get enough water in their elevated, airy locations.

EXPERT ADVICE
Plants that need lots of water should be watered from above and below.

EXPERT ADVICE
Increasing surrounding humidity is no substitute for watering.

EXPERT ADVICE
Immersion baths also help when the root ball has dried out.

What About Vacation?

Overview

Tips for People Who Water Too Much

Always water after doing the thumb test.
Water into the plant saucer instead of the pot.
Place gravel or vermiculite in the plant saucer.
Choose plants that require plenty of water.

Tips for People Who Water Too Little

Use clay pots rather than plastic ones.
Irrigate using clay watering posts.
Put the plants into an immersion bath from time to time.
Choose plants that don't need much watering.

Clay Watering Posts

Watering posts that are closed or filled with water are stuck into the plant's soil. Water is provided to the plant's substrate through the porous clay. The clay post is connected to a reservoir by a tube so that water is continually supplied to the plant. The plant can also absorb as much water as it needs. One watering post is adequate for small pots; larger ones need at least two. Using this system, it is possible to leave for a weekend or even a week. This is also a good system for people who don't like to water.

Improved Watering Post System

Plants with extensive leaf mass need plenty of water, and this is an opportunity to improve on the watering post system. In each pot, don't place just one watering post, but two or three. In addition, put the pot into a large plastic bag that reaches about four inches (10 cm) over the top of the pot, and close it tightly around the shoot with clothespins to minimize evaporation from around the root ball. Keep the shoots and the leaves free of the plastic bag. Put about an inch (2 cm) of water into the bag. Large plants can be left for up to two weeks with this setup.

EXPERT ADVICE
Clean the watering posts and tubes regularly so that they don't become clogged.

Even if you don't find someone to take care of your plants, there's no need to pass up your vacation.

Watering Mat on the Sink

In specialty shops you can get a watering mat that's ideal for a few days' absence, and for plants that don't need too much water. The pots are placed on top of the mat, one end of which reaches into a sink that's filled with water. The mat absorbs as much water as it can, and the plants, which stand directly on top of the mat, draw the water they need from the mat in proximity to the roots.

Place the plants close together to reduce the evaporation rate.

Wicks

Irrigating plants using special wicks available in shops works on the same principle of absorption: Use a large needle to work the moist wick through the drain hole and the substrate, up to the surface of the soil, wind it around the plant two to three times, cover it over with a little soil, and pat it down gently. Let the lower end of the wick hang in a container of water.

Place the reservoir of water at about the same height as the flowerpot.

Placing Plants in a Reservoir

If you plan on being away from home for only a few days, you can place the well-watered plants into a pan containing vermiculite and half filled with water. It also helps to put damp newspapers into the space between the pots. It's best to keep the plants slightly shaded to reduce water consumption. For that purpose you can close the Venetian blinds partway or place the plants out of direct sunlight.

EXPERT ADVICE
Before going on vacation, check to be sure that your watering method is working properly.

EXPERT ADVICE
Water your plants once again on the day you leave.

Accessories for Watering

	Application	Tips
	**Watering** For watering larger plants, a watering can that holds five to ten quarts/liters of water and has a short spout is fine. For smaller potted plants, a small watering can with a long pouring spout is more appropriate.	As soon as you're finished watering, fill the watering can again so that the water can sit and reach room temperature. Clean the inside of the can regularly to keep it from building up film.
	**Misting** It's important to maintain high humidity for plants that come from the humid tropical rain forest by misting them regularly. When cuttings are used for propagation in plant terrariums and bottle gardens, misting replaces watering.	Mist only with lime-free water at room temperature. Choose a mister that uses a simple pump mechanism to create a buildup of pressure before misting.
	**Irrigating with Watering Posts** Irrigating with watering posts is ideal for beginners and people who don't have much practice watering plants, for the plants will absorb exactly the amount of water that they need. This is also a good way to irrigate when you're away on vacation.	Check the water level in the reservoir frequently. The containers that hold the water will develop algae rather quickly; use dark glass, and wash out or change the reservoir fairly regularly.
	**Irrigating with Mats** Plants can easily be left for a weekend on a watering mat on the sink.	Before you leave, water the plants once again; make sure that excess water can run off rather than build up.

Anyone who has more than two or three houseplants needs more than a single watering can.

	Application	Tips
	**Increasing Humidity** In heated and dry rooms, you can increase humidity by using pans filled with vermiculite or gravel and water, or clay coasters or humidifiers that are placed on top of heaters.	With tropical plants that need high humidity, humidifiers are no substitute for regular watering.
	**An Inexpensive Way to Soften Water** For plants that need lime-free water, the quickest and easiest way to soften tap water is to boil it in a teakettle.	Before filling the watering can, let the boiled water cool off properly so that the lime can settle out.
	**A More Costly Method for Softening Water** Water that contains lime can also be softened, at a slightly higher cost than boiling, by using special ion exchangers.	Ion exchangers need to be replaced fairly frequently. Use only ion exchangers from garden supply shops.
	**Collecting Rainwater** Rainwater contains no lime; however, it may contain pollutants from the roof. Therefore, don't collect the first water that runs off the roof.	Don't gather rainwater in large cities, or near industrial sites or highways. Always keep the rain barrel covered. Don't use rainwater that has been standing too long in the barrel.

Fertilizing

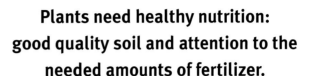

**Plants need healthy nutrition:
good quality soil and attention to the
needed amounts of fertilizer.**

Properly fertilized plants grow better and remain healthier. This sounds like a self-evident statement, but unfortunately, it's frequently overlooked.

The Right Food for Each Plant

Different plants need different fertilizers. Green plants, for example, need different fertilizer than blooming plants do. That's because producing leaves requires a different nutritional composition than growing stalks and leaves. Even special plant groups such as Cactuses, Orchids, and Azaleas, and plants grown in hydroponics, have very specific nutritional requirements; all of them are addressed by products that are available through gardening shops.

As long as you are attentive to using a high-quality product enriched with the necessary trace elements, you can be sure that you are feeding your plants properly. Here's an applicable rule of thumb: the warmer and brighter a plant is kept, the more fertilizer it needs.

There's More to Soil than Just Dirt

Just as there are different types of fertilizers (see page 34), there are different kinds of potting soils. If you are not practicing hydroponics (see page 62), your plants will grow best if you provide them with the appropriate type of soil (see page 32). That's essential for them to thrive, because that's the only way they can take in the right amounts of the nutrients they need.

A Time for Growing and a Time for Resting

During the growing season—generally the time from around the beginning of March to the beginning or middle of October—plants need more nutrition. For the home gardener, that means regular fertilizing or using a long-lasting fertilizer. For many plants, during the rest period, when there is less daylight—from around October through the end of February—fertilizing generally will have to be interrupted, or at least cut back.

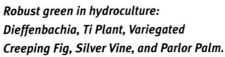

Robust green in hydroculture:
Dieffenbachia, Ti Plant, Variegated
Creeping Fig, Silver Vine, and Parlor Palm.

Growth Requires Nourishment

Plants let you know when they need food: they don't grow as quickly, their leaves lose their color, they cease to bloom, and they lose their leaves. Plants especially need
▶ Nitrogen for general growth
▶ Phosphorus for production of flowers and fruit
▶ Potassium for better tissue development
In addition there are a number of essential trace elements such as iron, copper, and manganese. If just one of these building blocks is missing, the plant can't continue to grow. And every plant group, sometimes even an entire species, has special fertilizer requirements (see page 32).

Different Types of Fertilizer
There are several forms of fertilizer available in the marketplace: liquid, powdered or granulated, in the form of fertilizer stakes and sticks, and long-lasting fertilizers. With time indoor gardeners will find out what type of fertilizer suits them best, and which products yield the best results.

Feeding Tips
▶ Always use fertilizers according to the manufacturer's instructions.

▶ Fertilize regularly.
▶ Remember that fast-growing plants such as Indoor Linden and Weeping Fig need more fertilizer than slow-growing plants like cactuses.
▶ Also consider that many plants need a rest phase, and little or no fertilizer during the winter months when the days are shorter.

Different Plant Substrates
Just as with fertilizers, plant substrates are very specific; they can be mixed from a variety of components:
▶ Growth-encouraging humus
▶ Clay, which helps regulate water and fertilizers
▶ Additives such as sand and polystyrene, which keep the mixture loose

Using Liquid Fertilizers
Liquid fertilizers are easy to measure, and are mixed with water for the plants.

For example, there are specialized substrates for Cactuses, Orchids, and Azaleas, for green plants, and for flowering plants; they are mixed in the best proportions of soil and fertilizers for any given plant. All these substrates depend on proper watering and fertilizing; good quality substrates are stable in their structure and don't clump up in the pot. Usually this higher quality also has a price. Most of the substrates you find in stores are mixed so that they are usable for a broad variety of houseplants, and they are marketed under many different names.

Growing Without Soil
Some plant specialties, which grow as epiphytes on the bark of forest giants, need no potting soil. All they need is a handful of moss or decayed plant material to attach to (e.g., some types of Orchids, Bromeliads, and ferns).

How About Using Your Own Compost?
Compost is a fine plant fertilizer in a garden, but for houseplants it can be used only if it's treated in advance with steaming hot water. That's the only way to kill weed seeds and germs that can cause disease, which are

The marketplace offers fertilizers in many different forms: as liquids, powders or granules, and in long-lasting forms such as tablets, stakes, and sticks.

always present in compost heaps, and keep them from harming the sensitive houseplants.

Repotting—a Must
Plants that are growing well naturally form strong root balls that eventually fill up the entire pot; that's the time to repot the plant into a larger container with new soil.

▶ Choose a new pot that's about an inch (2 cm) larger than the previous one.
▶ The best time for repotting is the end of February or the beginning of March, when the plants will soon experience a new growth impulse as light intensity increases.

Growing in Clay Aggregates
One fairly pleasant and easy way to grow houseplants is hydroponics, in which the plants grow in a special vermiculite substrate. They don't need to be repotted as frequently, and they can be given plenty of water and fertilizer.

There's More to Soil than Just Dirt

Overview

Growing Without Soil

Bromeliads
Tillandsia

Need Special Substrates

Cactuses
Orchids
Citrus Plants

Prefer Acidic Soils

Azaleas
Begonias
Coleus
Flamingo Flower
Norfolk Island Pine

Tolerate Potting Soil with Lime

Agave
Clustered Bell Flower
Sansevieria

Potting Soil

A good quality potting soil, also refer-red to in stores as potting medium, is a good choice for most houseplants. These soils have a consistent texture, with a certain amount of clay added, and they are free of contaminants and weed seeds. High-quality soil usually contains some fertilizer, so newly potted plants will need to be fertilized only after about six weeks.

Special Substrates

Some types of plants need special substrates; Azaleas, for example, need a substrate with a low pH; Orchids need a substrate that's very permeable to water and air; Cactuses grow best in a fairly sandy substrate that's porous and nutrient poor. You can get these special substrates in any gardening supply store.

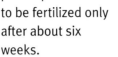

The most important consideration in repotting plants is the right substrate; however, aeration and drainage are also important.

Vermiculite
Vermiculite can absorb water and keep the root balls of plants moist for a longer time. Since it has a coarse texture, it allows for good aeration so that the plant's roots don't drown.

Gravel for Drainage
In repotting, a layer of gravel is first put into the pot; it provides a layer for drainage and adds weight to the pot, thereby making it more stable.

Well-Aerated Plant Substrate
For plants that like a loose soil that's easy to warm up, you can mix into the potting soil some coarse ingredients such as sand or polystyrene in the ratio of one to three. This provides for better aeration in the substrate and helps excess water run off without collecting.

Clay Shards Prevent Washouts
To keep the substrate from washing out when you water the plant, you can cover the drainage hole in the pot with several shards from a clay pot before filling the container with soil. Nowadays people no longer mix in clay shards with the soil, as was formerly recommended. It's true that the shards aerate the soil and help to keep it moist. However, they create a hazard when you work in the soil, so it's better to use vermiculite instead.

CROSS REFERENCE
Watering: pages 22–23
Watering During Vacation: pages 24–25

CROSS REFERENCE
Propagating: pages 64–67

CROSS REFERENCE
Repotting: pages 42–43

Different Types of Fertilizers

Overview

Fertilizing Bromeliads

Apply fertilizer solution for green plants according to manufacturer's instructions. Mix one part with ten parts soft water and feed to plant. For misting or filling the leaf well, cut this solution to 50 percent with soft water.

Fertilizing Ferns

A fourth of the concentration of the usual commercial fertilizers is adequate.

Fertilizing Cactuses

Use fertilizer for cactuses or a 25 percent solution of commercial fertilizer for green plants.

Fertilizing Orchids

Use fertilizer for orchids or a quarter to a maximum of half the usual commercial fertilizer for green plants.

Liquid Fertilizers

Liquid fertilizers are simply mixed with water. Never fertilize directly onto dry substrate; rather, moisten the substrate before fertilizing.

Before mixing granulated or powdered fertilizers with the water, it's a good idea to dissolve them slightly in a little water. This solution can then be stirred into the appropriate amount of water according to the manufacturer's instructions. When using liquid fertilizers, observe carefully the food needs of your plants.

Fertilizer Stakes

Fertilizer stakes make it easy to fertilize, because they work over several months and you don't run the risk of fertilizing too much or too little. In the springtime, push the fertilizer stakes into the outer edge of the substrate so that they are completely covered. The number of stakes is dictated by the type of plant and the size of the pot. It's important to be sure that the stakes get watered along with the plant so that they dissolve and release their nutrients little by little.

EXPERT ADVICE
Better to fertilize too little than too much!

During their growth period, houseplants have to be supplied regularly with nutrients. Long-term fertilizers are easy to use.

Fertilizer Sticks/Tablets

Fertilizer sticks and tablets provide the plant with necessary nutrients slowly and over a fairly long time. These long-acting fertilizers are also given in the springtime. Use the handle of a spoon or a stick to push the fertilizer deep into the substrate. If several servings of food are needed for larger plants or groups of plants, the sticks or stakes are shared equally among the plants.

Organic Fertilizers

Organic fertilizers such as horn meal can also be used as long-acting ferti-lizers. The right amount of fertilizer is added under the substrate when the plants are repotted in the spring, or a layer of fertilizer is spread on top of the soil (see illustration above).

This procedure is well suited to plants that like to feed on fertilizers, such as Hibiscus and Pot Rose, as well as for houseplants that need to be repotted only every two to three years.

Changing Nutrient Batteries

For plants grown in hydroponics the nutrient battery with a long-acting fertilizer needs to be changed from time to time (approximately every three months) so that the nutrients that haven't been used don't build up and damage the tender plant roots.

Note: There are long-acting fertilizers for hard and for soft water; choose the right type of fertilizer for the type of water you have.

CROSS REFERENCE
Repotting: pages 42–43

CROSS REFERENCE
Hydroponics: pages 62–63

Recognizing and Eliminating Plant Care Mistakes

Problem	Description/Cause	Remedy and Tips
	**Legginess (Excessive Growth)** The plant shoots are thin and long. Individual leaves are spaced very far apart. The leaves are usually yellow or light green. The plant has not been getting enough light.	Give the plant more sunshine. Cut the long shoots back to about an inch. It's a good idea to repot in new soil.
	**Sunburn Spots** The leaves have brown spots; they may be small and lentil shaped, or long and oval. The leaves have become burned by strong sun and/or water on the leaves.	Damaged leaves don't repair themselves. Protect the plant from direct sunshine; don't leave water on the leaves; don't mist in the sunshine; let plants that are placed outdoors get used to the sun gradually.
	**Drooping Leaves and Shoots** Leaves and shoots hang down loosely, even though the soil is moist enough. Either the plant has been over-fertilized or has suffered root damage by being kept too cool.	Remove the plant from the pot and wash off the roots; trim off damaged roots and repot in fresh substrate; put it in a place where the soil will stay warmer.
	**Dropping Leaves or Buds** The plant suddenly starts to drop leaves that are still green and/or buds, or the leaves turn brown along the edges, curl, and fall off. The plant doesn't have enough humidity.	The plant needs higher humidity or misting. Don't mist blooming plants on the leaves or buds.

Many problems with houseplants are caused by the wrong location or improper watering and fertilizing.

Problem	Description/Cause	Remedy and Tips
	**Yellow Leaves on Weeping Fig** The plant's leaves turn yellow and drop off in great numbers; even green leaves fall off. Weeping Fig reacts to draft, changes in location, and too moist or too dry root ball by dropping its leaves.	Protect the plant from draft; don't continually change its location; check for excessive watering or dry root ball.
	**Noticeably Light-Colored Leaves** Leaves are conspicuously lighter green and seem faded. Cause may be too sunny a location or excessive fertilizer.	Check the plant's location requirements and change to a shadier spot if necessary. Don't give too much fertilizer at one time; less fertilizer more frequently is better.
	**Yellowing of Leaves (Chlorosis)** New leaves in particular turn yellow between the veins so that the veins stand out green. The plant is suffering from iron deficiency caused by excessively high lime content in the substrate.	For immediate help, administer fertilizer containing iron; it's best to repot the plant in fresh soil and use water with reduced lime content.
	**Completely Root-Bound Plant** The plant is completely root bound and even pushes soil out of the pot. The plant has become too large for the pot.	Repot the plant in new substrate and a larger pot. Regularly repot or transfer to hydroponics, which requires less frequent repotting.

Proper Care

Given an appropriate location and the right amount of watering, most houseplants require little additional care.

One of the most important requirements for healthy houseplants is a watchful eye. People who communicate daily with their plants are quick to see when something is not right.

Golden Rules

Here are some basics of houseplant care:
▶ Give the plants plenty of room.
▶ Most plants like bright locations, but not in full sun and not too hot (around 72°F/22°C); they also don't like draft.
▶ In the wintertime, many plants prefer a cool, bright location.
▶ Plants with a large leaf mass lose lots of water through transpiration and require higher humidity. They need to be misted fairly often.
▶ Spray only with lime-free water at room temperature.
▶ With most plants, the root ball should be neither entirely wet nor dry; use the thumb test frequently.
▶ Fertilize regularly in two- to four-week intervals during the growth period in the springtime and the summer, or fertilize once in the spring using a long-acting fertilizer.
▶ Don't fertilize during the winter rest period, and water less frequently.
▶ If the root ball becomes root bound, transfer plant to a larger pot with fresh substrate in the spring.
▶ Remove wilted plant parts regularly.
▶ Leafy plants should have one good shower per year to get the dust off the leaves.

Light or Intensive Care

For plants that require minimal care, such as Ivy, Split Leaf Philodendron, Spider Plant, Rubber Tree, Sansevieria, Parlor Palm, and Yucca, the plant care tips given above are entirely adequate.

For plants that need lots of care, such as Azaleas, Orchids, green plants with variegated leaves, and many blooming plants, you need to know and adhere to their precise requirements so that you can enjoy them for a long time.

Foliage plants don't have to be just green, as this distinctive arrangement clearly shows.

Some Care Required

Everyone would like to have a green thumb. Then we could have any plant we wanted, and the eternal insecurity of "Now what am I doing wrong?" would cease to plague us.

Read the Instructions

Every plant offered for sale, no matter how exotic, comes with a complete description of the types of conditions under which it grows best.

▶ When you buy a plant, always ask for its precise name, and for instructions on how to care for it if the appropriate label isn't present in the pot.

▶ Many gardening centers have little brochures with directions on caring for the most common types of plants; ask for one.

▶ The little handbooks that describe the most common houseplants in greater or lesser detail can also be helpful.

▶ If you want to become more involved with houseplants, it will be worth your while to get a thorough book on the topic (see the suggestions on page 152).

Check the Location and Water Quality

Compare the chosen locations of your plants with the directions that came with them. Do they offer the plant the right light conditions? How is the temperature? Does the plant have enough space? Also note that many plants need a different location in the summer than in the winter.

Check the quality of the water you use on the plants. How hard is your tap water, and how much water hardness will your new arrival tolerate?

Observe Your Plants

If you don't yet have much experience caring for houseplants, you should keep a close watch on your new acquisitions during the first weeks; that way you will quickly detect any changes in the plants and be able to deal with them.

Large, coarse leaves should always be wiped free of dust with a damp cloth.

▶ Do the thumb test every two or three days. Is the substrate moist enough?

▶ Take a good look at the leaves. Have they changed in any way? Are they still taut and firm, or are they limp? Has their color changed? Are they yellow or brown at the tips?

▶ Check the buds of blooming plants. Are they continuing to grow? Are they opening, or have they stagnated in their growth?

▶ Also take a look at the underside and the joints of the leaves. Might there be any pests present?

Recognizing and Eliminating Hazards

Diseases caused by animal pests, bacteria, and fungi can make it hard to keep our plants looking beautiful. And the worst part is that they quickly spread to other plants. It's often tedious, time consuming, and futile to combat them. Therefore, it's worthwhile to inspect very carefully and check the leaves (for fungal infestation), the tops and undersides of leaves (for scale insects), new shoots (for aphids), stalks (for fungal infestation), and substrate surface (for thrips and whiteflies). The sooner the infestation or illness is recognized, the more quickly you can begin to combat it.

In addition to watering and fertilizing, plant care involves misting, cutting back, repotting, and propagating.

Houseplants Throughout the Year

Plant care varies somewhat according to the time of year. Here's a brief overview:

▶ Spring

Repot or renew the top layer of soil as needed, and provide long-term fertilizer; cut back plants, move plants from cool to warmer locations, tidy up, and check for pests and diseases; make cuttings and divide plants that have grown too large; start fertilizing plants that have not been repotted; water and mist regularly.

▶ Summer

Protect plants from direct sun; place potted plants on porch or balcony; tie up or stake new shoots; water and mist more frequently; fertilize regularly (if no long-term fertilizer was used in the spring); wash under the shower from time to time.

▶ Autumn

Gradually cut back on fertilizing, watering, and misting; cut back and neaten up plants before winter; prepare for cultivation of bulbs.

▶ Winter

Don't give much water to plants kept in cool places; increase humidity in rooms affected by central heating; be on the watch for pests; bring bulb plants inside in January or February.

Spring—Time for Repotting

Overview

Materials

New pot about three inches (4 cm) larger in diameter
An appropriate plant saucer or cachepot (outer pot)
Appropriate potting soil
Organic fertilizer or long-term fertilizer
Clay shards or vermiculite

Tools

Watering can
Garden shears or large knife for shortening roots or root ball

Time

For smaller plants, about 15 minutes per plant; with large plants, about 30 minutes

Time for Repotting

Spring (March–April)

Repotting

To repot, tip the pot and support the top of the root ball and the stems with your hand. If the root ball doesn't come free, carefully tap the outside of the pot on the edge of a table and pull on the lower (thickest) part of the plant stem. In particularly difficult cases, break the pot away from the roots.

Getting Ready to Repot

Loosen up the roots and shorten them about an inch (2–3 cm); with very large specimens, use a large knife to cut about an inch (2–3 cm) from the root ball. Set clay pots into water an hour or two before repotting.

Providing Good Drainage

To avoid excess moisture and inadequate aeration of the root ball, put two or three fairly large clay shards or a layer of vermiculite over the drainage hole.

**In the spring, at the start of the growing season,
plants that have outgrown their pots need to be transplanted
into larger containers with fresh soil.**

Put in Substrate and Fertilizers

The drainage layer for large plants needs to be thicker than for smaller ones; it's a good idea to cover it with a piece of fleece, and then about an inch (2–3 cm) of plant substrate.

If you want to use long-lasting fertilizer, put in about half a handful of horn shavings, mix them with the substrate, and put another inch or so (2 cm) of substrate over that so that the plant roots don't come into direct contact with the fertilizer salts.

Put the Plants In

Check to see that the plants will fit into the new pot: the root ball should be about a half-inch (1–2 cm) under the rim of the pot so that later on the water won't run over the edge. If needed, add or remove substrate. Then set the ball into the middle of the pot so that there's about an inch (2 cm) of space around it. Fill the empty space with substrate and tamp it down firmly; as you do, make sure that the plant remains standing straight.

Forming a Watering Trench

Add plant substrate to cover the old root ball (to a maximum of a half-inch/ 1 cm), and then press once again on the start of the roots and on the sides. Finally, use your thumbs to form a half-inch (1 cm) deep watering trench. If necessary, insert a brace or support and tie the plant to it. Water profusely and let the excess water run off.

If no long-term fertilizer has been used, don't fertilize in the following two to four weeks, since the soil usually comes already fertilized.

CROSS REFERENCE
Adding long-term fertilizer
page 35

CROSS REFERENCE
Tying up plants, page 44

Occasional Measures

Overview

Materials

sturdy plant stake made of
bamboo, metal, or wood
shoot support
plant ring
florist's wire
fresh potting soil

Tools

garden or household shears
sturdy digging fork or small
garden rake
damp wool fabric

Time Frames

Tidying up, cutting back
    15–20 minutes
Tying up:
    Depending on plant size
    15–30 minutes
Showering a Plant:
    15–20 minutes
Wiping off Leaves:
    30–60 minutes
Renewing Topsoil:
    approximately 20 minutes

Tidying Up a Plant

Wilted flowers or leaves that have turned yellow or brown look unattractive, interfere with new growth at that spot, and may lead to illnesses such as fungal infestations. Therefore it's a good idea to get rid of them as soon as possible.

It's easy enough to pick the wilted flowers off, but it's even better if you cut off the blooms and leaves along with their stalk from the rest of the shoot. The cut should be at the nearest point of green vegetation—in other words, where the plant will sprout next.

Staking Up

Plant stakes made of bamboo or metal provide a secure hold for tall plants that have a single stem; the stakes are threaded along the stalk from above and through the leaf stems. Insert the stake as deep as possible near the apex of the root ball to keep the plant straight and steady. Then secure the main stalk to the stake, using plastic-coated plant rings. The leaves should still be free to grow beyond the rings.

EXPERT ADVICE
It's a good idea to stake several strong shoots individually.

Given an appropriate location, proper watering, and the right amount of fertilizer, additional plant care is minimal.

Showering

Plants with large or leathery leaves should be showered at least twice a year with water at room temperature; this rids the leaves of dust, which unfortunately collects even on plants, and which eventually blocks the plant's pores.

Sticky films and aphids can be removed using a powerful stream of water. In so doing, though, you should hold your hand under the leaf being treated so it doesn't get torn off by the spray.

Renewing Soil

Large plants and hanging plants don't need to be repotted every year unless the root ball is permeated by tomentum. Changing the top layer of soil is usually all that's needed:

Using a small, short-pronged fork or a small plant rake, carefully loosen up the top layer, rake the loose substrate together, and remove it. Then add new substrate, press it down a little, and water it—that's all there is to it!

Cut Off Brown Leaf Tips

Palms that have been kept too dry quickly develop brown leaf tips. You can simply cut off the brown tips. Don't cut into the green part of the leaves, but leave just a fraction of an inch of the brown.

Cutting Back

Leafless plants and plants that should grow bushier need to be cut back significantly when they are repotted in the spring. They are cut where the leaves or a new shoot appears.

CROSS REFERENCE
Combating pests: pages 48–49

CROSS REFERENCE
Repotting plants: pages 42–43

CROSS REFERENCE
Caring for palms: page 57

Identifying and Treating Diseases

Overview

Fungal Infestations

- Leaf Spots
- Powdery Mildew
- Gray Mold
- Cactus Stem Rot
- Tuber Rot (Cyclamen)
- Rust
- Stem Rot
- Root Rot

Preventive Measures

- Water only on root ball, not on leaves and blooms.
- Don't keep plants too moist, especially ones with soft leaves.
- Especially in cool rooms, leave no water standing on leaves.
- Cut off damaged plant parts.
- Promptly remove parts of the plant that fall off.

Gray Mold

Plants with soft, thin-skinned shoots and leaves that are kept too moist are often affected by a fungus (*Botrytis*) that is first recognizable as a gray, downy layer of mold on the stems, and subsequently spreads out to leaves and blooms. Remove the diseased plant parts, place the plants in a light and airy location, and cut back on watering.

Powdery Mildew

Affected plant parts, especially the tops of leaves and blooms, are covered with a floury layer that starts out white but becomes brownish as the infestation increases. Plant parts that are severely affected dry out and eventually die. Remove the affected plant parts as quickly as possible and put the plant into a light, dry, and airy location.

The most common houseplant diseases are caused by fungi that mostly affect plants that are weakened or damaged.

Leaf Spots

With weakened houseplants, especially green plants such as Dragon Plant, types of Ficus, Croton, and Kangaroo Vine, as well as Flamingo Flower, a whole array of fungi can settle on or in the leaves and cause reddish, brown, or light spots of varying sizes.

Remove the affected leaves and provide the plant with the location and the growing conditions that are best suited to it.

Basal Rot

Stem base rot is caused mostly by *Fusarium* or *Phytium* fungi that attack the plant where the stem joins the root ball. Particularly affected are plants with succulent stems (such as begonias) and cuttings. The leaves and shoots of diseased plants show signs of wilting and hang down limp even though the substrate is sufficiently moist. Closer inspection reveals that the base of the stem is brown in color.

Affected plants should be discarded.

Root Rot

Root rot occurs mainly when the plants are kept too moist and cold for a fairly long period of time and the roots become weakened or damaged. Root damage is recognizable first as poor plant growth, which can eventually lead to the plant's death.

Remove diseased plants from their pots, cut away the damaged roots, rinse off the root ball, pot the plant in new substrate, and keep the root ball drier and warmer.

EXPERT ADVICE
Fungicides (fungus killers) should be used only in extreme cases.

EXPERT ADVICE
Always check the roots carefully when you repot a plant.

Identifying and Combating Pests

Overview

Mechanical Ways to Combat Pests

With minor infestation, pick off pests one at a time.
Rinse off plants under running water or cut off affected plant parts.
Wash off or mist with a soap solution.

Put Up Some Flypaper

Harmful flying insects can be caught with nontoxic flypaper.

Using Beneficial Insects

Gardening shops offer certain types of beneficial insects that can be introduced to help control pests:
Lacewings for aphids, ichneumon flies for whiteflies, predatory mites for spider mites, Australian lady bugs for mealy bugs.

Aphids

Aphids (greenflies) are usually green colored, but there are also yellow, brownish, red, and black varieties. These pests invade mostly weakened plants and like a warm, dry environment. These sap sucking creatures cause growth irregularities, since they prefer to settle on fresh shoots.

With minimal infestations, mechanical removal and misting with a soap solution are effective. With heavier infestations chemical spray may be necessary.

Scale Lice

By far the toughest pests are scale lice. They mostly infest plants that have firm leaves and a smooth, waxy upper surface. They are recognizable as flat, light brown to brown oval, immobile little discs.

With a minor infestation, pick the creatures off or wash off and mist the leaves with a soapy solution—including the undersides of the leaves. In cases of more persistent infestation, mist with a special insecticide spray or put in plant protection suppositories, which work from within.

EXPERT ADVICE
Use lacewings as a biological remedy.

EXPERT ADVICE
Repeat remedy after a few days.

Pest infestations may be caused by improper local conditions such as excessively dry, warm air and inadequate ventilation.

Mealy Bugs

What appear at first glance to be little cotton balls sticking to the branches and/or leaves are usually mealy bugs. Closely related to pernicious scale, they can be combated in the same way—except instead of misting, it's best to paint them with soapy water and then rinse them off. If the mealy bug infestation doesn't diminish after two or three months, you may as well discard the plant.

Red Spider Mites

Tiny webs flecked with little dots between leaves or at the tips of shoots and branches are unmistakable signs of a spider mite infestation. This occurs especially when plants are too dry, too warm, and kept in a drafty area.

First shower the plant to remove some of the pests mechanically. Then water the plant well, put a plastic bag over the plant and secure it so that it's airtight around the pot, and let it stand for a few days (see page 50); then give the plant another shower and set it in a bright and humid location.

Whitefly

Whiteflies occur especially in warm, dry areas and reproduce explosively. The adult creatures commonly congregate on the tips of shoots; their larvae, however, remain on the undersides of leaves and suck juices from the plant. When the plant is moved, the pests fly away conspicuously.

Adult whiteflies can be caught with flypaper; the larvae are difficult to combat, however. Ichneumon flies may be the best remedy.

EXPERT ADVICE
Keep pesticides out of the reach of children!

EXPERT ADVICE
In case of spider mite infestation, you can also introduce predatory mites.

EXPERT ADVICE
If you introduce beneficial insects for pest control, don't use any pesticides.

Combating Living Pests

Procedure	Description	Pests
	**Using Flypaper** Flypaper board is coated with glue; it can be hung in the plant's leaves or staked into the substrate.	Helpful in combating flying pests such as aphids, thrips, sciarid flies, and adult whiteflies
	**Spraying with Soapy Solution** Spraying with a soapy solution aids in the removal of pests. The solutions consists of 1 tablespoon of liquid soap, 1 tablespoon of methylated spirits, and one liter of warm water. Repeat the procedure fairly often over the course of three days.	Aphids, pernicious scale, and mealy bugs
	Set Up a Plant Sauna This is appropriate only for leafy plants. Water the plant, then cover it with a large, clear plastic bag; secure it airtight around the pot and let stand for a few days. This doesn't kill the pests, but it keeps them from reproducing.	Spider mites and thrips
	**Immersing a Plant** For mild infestations, it's often adequate to rinse the plant several times in succession under lukewarm water or dip it headfirst into a bucket of lukewarm water.	Aphids, spider mites, thrips

Unfortunately, houseplants are always subject to pest infestation. But bludgeoning the pests to death with chemicals is not the right solution.

Procedure	Description	Pests
	Introduce Beneficial Insects Beneficial insects such as Australian lady bugs (see picture), lacewings, or predatory mites are natural enemies of harmful insects. They eat them or parasitize them.	Aphids, spider mites, thrips, mealy bugs
	Fortifying Plants Plants should be adequately fortified so that pests don't have a chance. To this end, you can add an aspirin to the plants' water from time to time, or give them egg water (leave some egg shells in water for a few days).	Aphids, scale lice, mealy bugs, thrips, sciarid flies, spider mites
	Onion-Garlic Extract An extract made from onions and garlic is an effective preventive measure: mince onions and garlic, cover with water, and let sit for several hours. Strain solution and mist plants two to three times per week.	Aphids, spider mites, thrips
	Mechanical Measures With minimal infestations that can be identified early by checking with a magnifying glass, you can often pick the pests off with your fingers or whisk them off with a toothbrush or a cotton swab.	Aphids, scale lice, thrips, mealy bugs

Special Care

**People who want to enjoy their
plants also need to see how they grow from
year to year and reproduce.**

Houseplants don't simply die if light, water, nutrients, and temperature are only marginally right for their requirements; however, you can't expect them to thrive and grow vigorously under those conditions.

Luxuriant Growth, Magnificent Blooms

Houseplants grow and thrive well and bloom magnificently only when their basic needs and special desires are addressed:

▶ What's the relative humidity? Does the plant prefer dry conditions, or does it like to be misted regularly?

▶ Which plants enjoy a "summer vacation" outdoors?

▶ Which plants need a resting period?

▶ What are the special considerations for winter?

Plant Care Begins at Time of Purchase

How a plant develops is influenced as early as point of purchase:

▶ Buy your plants from specialty shops and get advice from the professionals any time you have questions.

▶ Buy plants (other than seasonal or short-lived flowering plants) as early as possible in the spring or summer; then the transfer from the shop to your home is not so drastic, since your house isn't heated and dry. In addition, in the winter the plants have to be carefully packed so that they stay warm in transit and escape damage from the cold.

▶ Take a good look at the plants: Do the leaves have good color? Can you see new growth? Look under the leaves to see if any pests have taken up residence.

▶ In choosing flowering plants, select specimens that have not yet fully bloomed, but that have set plenty of fresh buds.

▶ Be sure that the root ball is not dried out, and that no moss or algae are present.

You can get hibiscus in many different colors as a long-stemmed or a normal, bushy plant.

More Enjoyment from Houseplants

People who enjoy houseplants will surely want more than short-lived flowering plants in their house. They will also want to surround themselves with plants that can stay in the same place year after year and keep filling out with new growth. They will bring plants to blooming every year and even keep some unusual plants, even though they may demand special care.

Last but not least, they will want to increase their stock little by little, either by purchasing new plants or by propagating plants that are already on hand.

Individualists All!

There are many examples of how varied the special requirements of individual and classes of houseplants are:

▶ Plants such as Maranta and Caladium (*Caladium bicolor* hybrids) need plenty of warmth and humidity.
▶ Cyclamen (*Cyclamen persicum*) and Azaleas (*Rhododendron simsii* hybrids) bloom for a longer time if they are kept in a bright but cool spot.
▶ A Christmas Cactus (Schlumbergera hybrids) that is setting buds must not be moved; otherwise it will lose its blooms.
▶ *Stephanotis floribunda* forms buds only after adequate winter rest.

▶ Passion Flower (Passiflora) sets more and better blooms after being cut back.

This list could go on and on. People who take a look at their plants every day and take care of their needs will develop a "green thumb."

Summer Vacation and Winter Rest

Many houseplants, such as Agave, Oleander, many citrus plants, and palms, thrive much better when they are placed outside during the summer (see pages 58–59). And many plants need a rest period (see pages 60–61) during which they are kept cooler, receive less watering, and get a break from fertilizing. For most houseplants, the rest period is in the winter; however, many plants such as winter bloomers take their rest in the summer.

Systematic Plant Care

If you want to make caring for your houseplants a little easier, especially with respect to regular watering and fertilizing, you might consider using hydroponics rather than soil culture (see pages 62–63). But the choice of plants that are best suited to hydroponics is rather restricted; many blooming plants won't thrive well, or will thrive only marginally, without soil. In addition, plants grown in hydroponics are usually a little more expensive to buy; just the same, for busy people who still want to surround themselves with living green, hydroponics is the best choice.

Getting More from Houseplants

It's especially exciting to produce offspring from your own houseplants. That's not just a way to get more houseplants; you'll also feel a good deal more attached to the plants that you have raised yourself. Houseplants can be propagated in the greatest variety of ways:

Remove Dust from Leaves
For plants that have hirsute leaves, you can use a small brush to remove dust easily.

Many houseplants can be propagated through cuttings, shoots, and dividing.

▶ by planting seeds
▶ by dividing larger plants
▶ by taking offsets, plantlets, runners, and bulbs, and
▶ with cuttings

Propagation in a Cold Frame

If you take so much pleasure in propagating your plants that you want to do more of it, it makes sense to get a special cultivation or propagation box from a garden supplies shop. These miniature greenhouses are available at different prices and in several designs; you could even build your own cold frame. Here are the important considerations:
▶ adjustable temperature (at least 65°F/18°C) so that cuttings root quickly;
▶ a transparent lid to act as protection against evaporation and maintain the right humidity inside the box. While using this type of box for propagating, be sure that
▶ there is always ventilation so there is no stagnant, moist air that could lead to rot;
▶ the plant substrate is not too moist, to keep the new roots from rotting; don't water the substrate, but mist it lightly.

CROSS REFERENCE
*Plant care accessories
pages 68–69*

Caring for Special Plants

Overview

Special Substrate Requirements

Azaleas:
> lime free, acidic substrate (Azalea or Rhododendron soil)

Leafy Cactuses:
> nutrient rich, air and water permeable soil (Cactus soil)

Ferns:
> not too rich substrate, well drained (check at gardening shops for the proper soil mix)

Cactuses from Desert and Rocky Regions:
> air and water permeable substrate; special cactus soil must be mixed with sand or fine gravel

Orchids:
> coarse, air and water permeable, nutrient rich substrate (Orchid soil)

Thorny Beauties

In the spring and summer, cactuses prefer sunny, warm, and well-ventilated places. In October, they prefer a bright but cool (38–55°F/6–12°C) and well-ventilated location. Use special cactus soil as a substrate, or potting soil with sand or polystyrene in a ratio of two to one. In spring and summer, provide water and cactus fertilizer every four weeks, and occasionally water thoroughly or immerse in water; don't water in the winter.

Azaleas

Keep Azaleas cool (around 65°F/18°C) and in a bright and well-ventilated place. Keep the root ball moist, and give the plant a weekly immersion bath; use only lime-free water. Fertilize once a week with Azalea or Rhododendron fertilizer. Regularly remove wilted leaves. From blooming time up to autumn, keep in a partially shaded spot on the porch or balcony; in autumn and winter, keep in a very cool (41–54°F/5–12°C), bright, and well-ventilated spot. Repot your Rhododendron every two to three years.

Azaleas, Ferns, Cactuses, Orchids, and Palms are among the plants that are exceptionally beautiful, but that also have very special requirements.

Orchids

The location requirements of Orchids vary from genus to genus; all of them, though, require a nighttime temperature that's lower than during the day, and a substrate that's very permeable and loose. It's best to use Orchid soil. Water only when the substrate becomes dry; mist frequently with lime-free water at room temperature. Add special Orchid fertilizer to the water only during the growth season. Repot when the substrate becomes decomposed or the plant outgrows the pot.

Respect the plant's rest period!

Palms

Palms, too, have very diverse location requirements; find out what they are when you acquire your palm. If the root ball is dry, water it with lime-free water at room temperature. It's better to water too little than too much. Soft-leafed types should be misted fairly frequently. During the growing period, fertilize every two weeks. Repot only when the soil becomes totally root bound; renew the top layer of the soil fairly often. Use potting soil as substrate; for older and larger plants, mix in a little loam.

Citrus Plants

In the spring and summer, citrus plants want to be in a sunny, warm, and well-ventilated area, preferably outdoors. Don't let the root ball dry out, but avoid waterlogging. Mist frequently with soft water; fertilize weekly. The plants should winter over at very cool temperatures (39–46°F/ 4–8°C); water more sparingly and withhold the fertilizer. Cut the plant back in the spring and repot it if the root ball has become completely root bound; otherwise, change the topsoil.

CROSS REFERENCE
Orchids, pages 102–103

EXPERT ADVICE
Young palms have very sensitive roots!

EXPERT ADVICE
Use potting soil mixed with loam (2 : 1).

Vacation on the Deck

Overview

For Shaded Places

Cyclamen, Ivy, Silver Spear, Parlor Palm

For Partially Shaded Places

Azaleas, Weeping Fig, Bromeliads, Dragon Plant, Silver Vine, Spider Plant, Piggyback Plant, Tradescantia, Fatsia

For Sunny Spots

Agave, Aloe, Banana, Jade Plant, Hibiscus, Cactuses, Yucca, Christmas Pepper, Umbrella Plant

Keep Indoors

Alocasia, Caladium, Peace Lily, Flamingo Flower, Croton, Maranta

Summer Vacation on the Deck

Many green plants, such as Weeping Fig, Dragon Plant, Spider Plant, Strawberry Begonia, and Fatsia, plus all Mediterranean container plants, like to take a vacation outdoors, especially if they already have luxuriant growth and lots of leaf mass. Most of them need partial shade and shelter from strong wind and pelting rain; a light summer rain is good for them, though. Large leafed, tall plants should be tied up to keep from falling over in a fairly strong wind. Take care that hanging plants don't dry out, and that they aren't too wet after a rain shower. Plants with large leaf mass usually use lots of water. It's therefore a good idea to water frequently, preferably in the evening hours after the sun has gone down.

Another method of providing adequate but not too much water involves watering through the plant saucer. Fill it full to the brim with water—even several times on a particularly sunny day. Pour off water that has not been absorbed after a half hour to avoid excessive moisture buildup.

EXPERT ADVICE
After a rain, check your plants outdoors for excess water.

Many houseplants thrive year-round if they can be outdoors and protected from summer wind and rain.

Azalea in Double Pot

Flowering Azaleas kept in a fairly cool location during the winter can be a feast for the eyes that lasts for weeks. In the summer it's best to put the plant outside in partial shade; it should be kept from drying out. You can put it into a second pot where, in contrast to other plants, you can easily leave a half inch of water. If you have a garden, you can even plant the azaleas in your flowerbed.

Plants on a Sunny Deck

Houseplants that like full sunshine can really soak it up in the summer. This is especially true for Mediterranean container plants such as Bougainvillea and citrus plants.

Note: Root balls dry out quickly in sunny locations, especially when there's a breeze. Many plants will need to be watered twice a day to get the moisture they need.

Palms on the Terrace

Palms and Yuccas should be placed outdoors in the summer, if possible. These plants have very different location requirements, though:

Coconut Palms (*Cocos nucifera*), Palm Ferns (*Cycas revoluta*), Mediterranean Fan Palms (*Chamaerops humilis*), and Yucca like full sun;

Parlor Palm (*Chamaedorea elegans*), Fishtail Palm (*Caryota mitis*), and Kentia Palm (*Howeia*) should have partial shade.

Be sure that wind doesn't damage the palm leaves, and that the plants remain solidly in place.

CROSS REFERENCE
Azalea care, pages 56 and 91

EXPERT ADVICE
Let houseplants adjust gradually to outdoor sunshine.

EXPERT ADVICE
Don't put palms outdoors before the middle of May.

Winter Rest Period

Overview

What to Do

Cutting back:
Cut back sparse or excessively large plants before the winter rest.

Tidying up:
Before putting the plants away, tidy them up by removing any dried parts.

Airing out:
On mild days with temperatures above freezing, occasionally air the plants out for a while to give them some fresh air.

Checking for Pests:
As early as January, pests may reappear; be particularly watchful for infestations of pernicious scale and aphids.

Moving Plants Indoors with a Dolly
To facilitate moving plants indoors, it's a good idea to use a dolly for large plants. There are also special carrying harnesses that allow two people to pick up and carry large pots. With thorny plants such as Agave, the sharp thorns should be covered before moving; you can put pieces of packing plastic over the sharp ends.

Wintering in a Bright and Cool Location
Plants that like to be cool in the winter include Bougainvillea (*Bougainvillea glabra*), Clivia, Common Fig (*Ficus carica*), Indoor Linden (*Sparmannia africana*), Mediterranean Fan Palm (*Chamaerops humilis*), and numerous cactuses; they all like it cool (around 50°F/10°C) but bright. In many houses that means a north-facing window, or even a bright staircase, whose height taller plants can use to good advantage.

Many houseplants need a winter rest period to gather their strength for the coming growth season.

Wintering in the Cellar

Many plants can even spend the winter in the cellar, as long as the location is absolutely frost-free and well ventilated. The room should have thermostatic climate control so that the temperature doesn't go below 32°F (0°C). Plants that lose their leaves in the winter, including such container plants as Parlor Maple (*Abutilon*) and Fuchsia, can be kept in areas of low light, including cellars that are equipped with no more than small windows.

Plants in a Greenhouse

Plants that need a bright but cool break in growth during the winter are best kept in a greenhouse or a cool winter garden. Dimensions are usually large enough to accommodate several large, overhanging container plants. Mediterranean plants can even be kept in a winter garden throughout the year. From spring through fall, it's sunny and warm, and it's cool and sunny in the winter.

Plants in a Winter Garden

Houseplants that need a fairly cool rest period during our winter months, such as Bougainvillea, Date Palms, Common Figs, Windmill Palm, Oleander, Abutilon, and Mediterranean Fan Palm, are best brought into an unheated, cool winter garden. Here even the largest and fullest plants have plenty of room, enough light, and the proper temperature.

EXPERT ADVICE
Periodically check up on plants kept in the cellar.

EXPERT ADVICE
Avoid stagnant air; air out the plants on a warm winter day.

Hydroponics: A Plant Care System

Overview

Materials

growing pot
water level indicator
vermiculite
waterproof hydroponics
container
nutrient battery

Time

about 45 minutes per plant

Time to Convert

**during growth phase from
spring to summer, except for
plants that have already set
buds**

Advantages of Hydroponics

Hydroponics is a plant care system in which the plant substrate is replaced by granulated clay known as vermiculite. Vermiculite is made from pure clay that is treated with a special heat process; the result is puffed up, porous balls of clay. Since this special substrate is chemically neutral, and it provides excellent ventilation and permeability to the roots, practically all plants will thrive in it. Plants in hydroponics have more water and nutrients available to them, so these are ideal conditions for regular growth. Even beginners in caring for houseplants can scarcely go wrong, since it's easy to tell by the water level indicator when more water is needed and when it's time to add fertilizer.

Hydroponics is a particularly good choice where regular care is difficult, as it is with people who are away a lot or are not home at regular times, and for offices that are empty during weekends.

CROSS REFERENCE
*Easy care with hydroponics
pages 106–107*

EXPERT ADVICE
Hydroponics is not appropriate for all houseplants.

Continual watering and fertilizing are passé with hydroponics; it's ideal for busy people who still want to be surrounded by refreshing green.

Transferring from Soil to Hydroponics

Relatively small plants that have been kept in soil are especially easy to transfer to hydroponics. The plant is removed from its pot, and the root ball is carefully rinsed under lukewarm water to free the roots of all clinging soil. This must be done very carefully, since later on any remnants of earth can lead to root rot in hydroponics. Then let the plant stand for a while longer in lukewarm water; cut off damaged or rotten root sections, and generally shorten the roots a bit.

Setting the Plant in Vermiculite

Fill the hydropot one-third full with moist vermiculite and insert the rinsed root ball. The plant should sit as high as it did in its previous pot. If the root ball is at the right level, then fill with vermiculite all around the root ball and up to the brim. Bump the pot a couple of times to settle the vermiculite a little. It's a good idea to keep the plant in a clear plastic bag for four weeks; the increased humidity and warmth will help it take root.

Providing Nutrients

Even with hydroponics there are various ways of providing nutrients. The easiest way is to use a nutrient battery for long-term hydroponics fertilizing, in which there are small, water-insoluble balls made of synthetic resin and filled with nutrients. The battery is simply inserted into the appropriate space under the growing pot. It will need to be replaced every four to six months.

EXPERT ADVICE
It's also a good idea to shorten the shoots a little.

EXPERT ADVICE
The size of the growing pot is determined by the waterproof cachepot.

CROSS REFERENCE
Changing nutrient batteries, page 35

Plant Propagation Through Cuttings

Overview

Leaf Cuttings

Cuttings that consist of an entire leaf (e.g., Begonias, African Violet, Dwarf Pepper) or part of a leaf (e.g., Strep-tocarpus, Sansevieria)

Top or Shoot Cuttings

Cuttings that consist of a shoot tip about three to four inches (8 to 10 cm) long; can be used with many herbaceous plants such as Philodendron, Painted Devil's Ivy, Hibiscus, Passion Flower, Desert Rose, and Indoor Linden.

Stem Cuttings

With plants that have fleshy shoot axils, the stem can also be used for cuttings; examples include Dieffen-bachia, Dragon Plant, Philo-dendron, and Yucca.

Propagating with Leaf Stalks

African violets are easy to propagate through leaf cuttings. Use a sharp knife to cut healthy and strong leaves, along with their stem, from the center of the plant. Carefully place the leaf cuttings and stems into moist potting soil in such a way that the leaves don't touch the substrate. After six to eight weeks little plants will develop at the base of the leaves.

Propagating with Leaf Cuttings

Search for a healthy Sansevieria leaf, cut it off, and divide the leaf crosswise into sections about two to three inches (5–8 cm) long. Let the pieces of leaf dry out, and then place them about an inch (2 cm) deep in potting soil in the direction of growth. Cover the pot with plastic wrap so the cut-tings won't be disturbed, and place in a loca-tion where the temperature is about 72°F (22°C). The first new plants will be visible after about six weeks.

Many houseplants can be propagated quite easily through cuttings. Try it and see how easy it is.

Letting Top Cuttings Sprout

With many houseplants, such as Spider Plant, Columnea, Tradescantia, and Zebrina, cuttings of tops and shoots easily sprout in water. The cutting simply must be kept warm and in a bright place. Take the cuttings from year-old, bloom-free shoots and place them into a glass of water at room temperature. Depending on the type of plant, it will take about four to six weeks until the shoots form roots and can be transferred to hydroponics or soil.

Rooting Umbrella Plants

Umbrella Plants root quickly in water. In its natural habitat, the banks of lakes and rivers, plant tops that break off and fall into the water grow roots and produce new, independent plants. That's easy to duplicate in a glass of water. Cut the top off along with a short section of stem, trim the leaves back by half, and place the top upside-down in a glass of water.

Propagating with Stem Cuttings

Dragon Tree, Yucca, and Dieffenbachia like to grow tall. With these plants, propagation and rejuvenation through stem cuttings works well.

With a Yucca, for example, first cut off the tuft of leaves and plant it so it will grow roots. The stem is cut into pieces about four to six inches (10–15 cm) long; each piece should have at least four axils. Let the cut ends dry out and set the pieces vertically in the direction of growth in potting soil. Place some clear plastic wrap around it to create a warm and bright place for the cutting.

EXPERT ADVICE
Cuttings root more readily in the light, warm season.

EXPERT ADVICE
See pages 68–69 for plant care accessories.

EXPERT ADVICE
Place stem cutting of Dieffenbachia horizontally on the substrate.

Propagating with Offshoots and Dividing

Overview

Offshoots (layering; runners)

This is a possible means of propagation for plants with long, flexible leaves that can be rooted; examples include Ivy, Spider Plant, Piggyback Plant, and Strawberry Begonia.

Plantlets

Plantlets are young plants that develop on the mother plant, as with Aloe and Clivia.

Offsets

Some houseplants, such as Mother of Thousands, form on the edges of their leaves small plants that already have roots; these can be planted right away.

Propagating by Dividing

Bushy plants (such as Peace Lily, Flamingo Flower, Parlor Palm, and Asparagus Fern) and plants that produce runners (such as Clivia and Agave) can easily be propagated through dividing.

Propagating Through Layering
To get new plants from runners, you can train the shoots of easy-rooting plants such as Ivy (*Hedera helix*) and Creeping Fig (*Ficus pumila*) into a pot of damp potting soil and secure them onto the substrate with a U-shaped piece of wire. As soon as the runners have produced roots, they also start to form new leaves. Then they can be cut from the mother plant.

Propagating with Runners
Some plants, such as Spider Plant (*Chlorophytum comosum*) and Piggyback Plant (*Tolmiea menziesii*) form runners on long stalks. These can be rooted in water or soil-like cuttings. But a more elegant solution is to put the runners into a pot of soil next to the mother plant. When the young plant takes root, the shoot that connects it to the mother plant is cut.

EXPERT ADVICE
Bobby pins work well for securing offshoots in a pot.

Cuttings are not the only way to propagate houseplants; you can also create offspring by rooting offshoots and by dividing plants.

Separating Plantlets

With Aloe, Bromeliads, Sansevieria, and many other houseplants, one or more small, new plants with a separate root system develop from runners that grow out right next to the mother plant.

Remove the plant from the pot and use a sharp knife to cut the plantlet off close to the mother plant. Put each plantlet into a pot by itself with moist potting soil.

Potting Offsets

With Mother of Thousands (*Kalanchoë daigremontiana*), many little baby plants grow between the serrations around the edges of the leaves; they form roots in the air and merely await the chance to come into contact with an appropriate substrate and take root. If the pot containing the mother plant is large enough, the babies take root right next to the mother plant as they grow older and fall off. But it's better to remove the little plants and put them into separate pots.

Dividing Plants

Bushy plants with several ground stems are most easily propagated by dividing the root stock. That's best done in the spring during repotting. Take the plant out of the pot and pull the root ball apart. With larger plants that have a stronger root ball, you'll have to use a sharp knife to cut it apart carefully. Each piece is then planted into its own pot with fresh substrate.

EXPERT ADVICE
Disinfect the knife before each new cut.

EXPERT ADVICE
Immediately remove damaged roots so they don't attract diseases.

Important Plant Care Accessories

Device	Purpose	Use and Tips
	**Pruning or Garden Shears, Knife** Get some smooth, handy, and easy-to-use pruning or garden shears, preferably with an articulated grip. A sharp knife will always come in handy in caring for plants.	For cutting back thick shoots and trimming bamboo support stakes. After purchase, clean the shears carefully and oil them.
	**Plant Stakes and Binding Material** You should always have plenty of plant stakes in various thicknesses and lengths on hand. Of course that also includes appropriate binding material (bast or plastic-covered wire twist ties).	For tying up and supporting long shoots. Wood plant stakes rot quickly; bamboo is a better choice.
	**Plant Rings** Various plant rings and ladders are very useful for tying up plants and bringing them into shape.	Plant rings are very good for keeping plants attached to a supporting stake without having to tie them securely.
	**Trellises and Arches** Trellises and arches come in various sizes, strengths, and thicknesses so that there is something for every taste and every plant.	Climbing plants need something to grow onto; special arches or other shapes lend themselves to personalized configurations.

A few good, basic plant care accessories are all you'll need.

Accessories	Purpose	Use and Tips
	**Clay Pots and Plant Saucers** You should always have a supply of clay pots and appropriate plant saucers on hand. Instead of plant saucers you can also use decorative cachepots.	You need pots and saucers for more than repotting in the springtime. From time to time pots may be tipped over by an unexpected wind, rambunctious children, or dogs.
	**Growing Frames** A small growing frame is essential for indoor gardeners who want to prop-agate plants; these frames provide the needed humidity and temperature conditions.	Growing frames are available in all sizes and shapes in gardening stores. You can also make one yourself quite easily.
	**Peat Pots/Potting Soil** A small supply of peat pots (for use with cuttings) and/or potting soil (for seeding and other propagation methods) is very useful.	Start by watering peat pots well, and then cover cuttings with clear plastic, since peat dries out very quickly. Use potting soil straight or mixed with a little sand (in a 3:1 ratio).
	**Winter Quarters** Anyone who has more than two or three houseplants sooner or later will need a bright, cool place for them to spend the winter, e.g., a roomy staircase or a bright cellar.	Even though the plants are resting for the winter, they should not be forgotten. This is the time when pests like to settle in. Therefore, don't crowd the plants too close to one another.

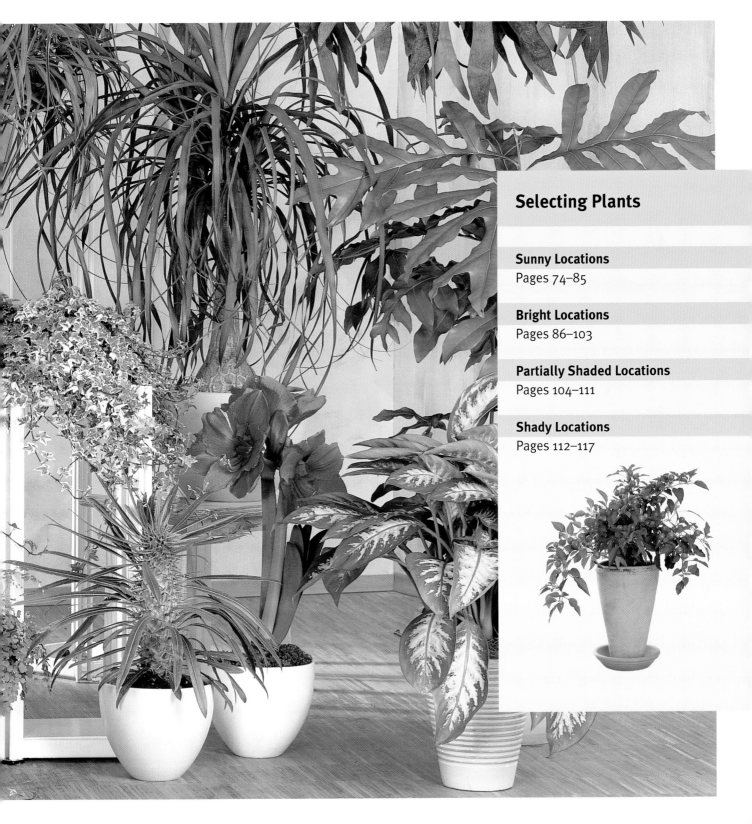

Selecting Plants

Selecting Plants

Sunny Locations
Pages 74–85

Bright Locations
Pages 86–103

Partially Shaded Locations
Pages 104–111

Shady Locations
Pages 112–117

Look for the Right Kinds of Plants

There you are in the gardening supply shop surrounded by all the green and blooming beauties, each one more beautiful than the next, and you don't know what to choose. Will the chosen plant thrive in my house? What kind of care does it require; can I—or anyone I bring it to—handle the plant all right?

It's a given that houseplants are a bit more demanding than our familiar old garden flowers. No wonder; they're not robust denizens of northern climes, but gracile and sometimes capricious beauties from foreign lands. But we surely do find them fascinating, and we are only too willing to bring one or more of them back home with us. To diminish somewhat the pain of deciding, the following pages will present in words and pictures the most common and easily cared for houseplants.

Plant Portraits

The following portraits provide you with an overview of the houseplants most frequently offered for sale in gardening shops, as well as a small selection of familiar container plants, cactuses, and orchids that are fairly easy to keep inside the house.
▶ Since the most important factor in caring for plants is the right location,

and especially enough light, the portraits have been divided into four categories:
—Plants for sunny locations
—Plants for bright locations
—Plants for partially shaded locations
—Plants for shaded locations
▶ Plants are grouped together in different categories within specific locations; for example blooming plants, leafy or foliage plants, large solitary plants, and trailing or climbing types.
▶ To see as wide a range as possible, look at the additional charts with alternative plants.

Grouping of Plant Portraits

Individual plant portraits are grouped in the following way:
▶ After the English names the internationally recognized scientific designations are given. Those are the names by which the plants are classified in catalogs and books.

Brand names are given in quotation marks but are used only rarely, for gardening shops and centers will usually go by the technical name rather than the special type listed on a label.
▶ The final information on plant height (or plant length in the case of hanging plants) and breadth will help indicate

the space that a plant will need after a few years.

The numbers provided should be regarded as averages, since there will be variations based on location and care given.
▶ The information about blooming times is likewise only a guideline, for it's often possible to keep many blooming plants in flower throughout the year.
▶ The fifth line provides information about the plant's life and may cover one or more years.

You may get many plants that are classified as blooming annual plants to last longer, but their growth may be sparse, and without professional help their blooming powers may be greatly reduced.
▶ The pictograms to the right will clarify at a glance the plant's most important characteristics and needs for care, water, and fertilizer.
▶ Then there is a notice about any noteworthy preference or obvious characteristic of the given plant.
▶ The remainder of the text deals with the colors and shapes of blooms, leaves, and fruits, location requirements, necessary care, and tips for arrangements.

Pictograms Used

 The plant requires little care.

 The plant requires a fair amount of care.

 The plant requires lots of care.

 Needs plenty of water every day. Use thumb test.

 Water moderately; use thumb test every two to three days.

 Water sparingly, but don't let plant dry out.

 Fertilize generously, about every one to two weeks.

 Fertilize moderately, around every four weeks.

 Fertilize sparingly; long-lasting fertilizers will be adequate.

 The plant is suited to hydroponics.

 The plant or its parts are poisonous or irritating to skin.

An unattractive window can be "repackaged" very effectively by using various houseplants and decorations.

Notes concerning descriptions of plants and their care:

Blooms/Fruits/Leaf Color and Form: These are the colors and shapes you are likely to find in a gardening center. Also check the photo. This will help you make a choice in line with your taste.

Location: Here again the location requirements are mentioned, with respect to the light, temperature, and humidity that the plant needs throughout the year, and which may be different in summer and winter.

Water, Fertilizer, and Care: Under these key words you will find tips on watering, fertilizing, and repotting, as well as other types of care.

Arrangements: Here you will find important tips on how and where the plant can be used in arrangements, as well as suggestions for combining it with other types of plants.

The last line contains some additional tips, cross references, and good combinations for arrangements on the windowsill or in the flowerpot.

CROSS REFERENCE
Thumb Test, page 22

Sunny Locations

Because of the high intensity of the sunshine, these locations can be extremely tricky ones for many houseplants.

Here's how the professionals define a sunny location: a place with a maximum light intensity of 3000 to 5000 lux and above.

Before you search for these conditions in your house or yard using a compass and lux meter, simply observe the movement of the sun over the course of a day. The greatest intensity of the sun's rays is where the sun shines directly into a room for several hours at midday.

Where's a Sunny Location?

Without a doubt the sunniest locations in a house are windowsills that face south, southwest, and west. Often these are windowsills in rooms where you prefer to be, such as living rooms or workrooms. In many homes, radiators are located beneath windows. That makes the windowsill warm and very dry in the winter. Sunny places in the yard and on a deck are often well sheltered by the

house or dividing walls, and these places may also be very warm.

What to Look For

Most of our houseplants don't tolerate extremes in conditions. Don't be amazed if certain types of plants lose their leaves in quantity, turn brown in many places, lose their color, or cease to bloom. Here's what to look for:
▶ Place on windowsills that are flooded with sunshine only plants that can tolerate lots of sun and heat.
▶ Carefully observe directions for watering.
▶ Air the plant out thoroughly two or three times a day.
▶ If possible, turn the thermostat down at night in the winter.
▶ Spray the plants fairly often — however, not in direct sunlight.
▶ Provide shade, if possible, around midday to reduce the intensity of the sun's rays.

Cactuses and succulents especially like sunny windowsills.

Colorful Plants on the Windowsill

Desert Rose
Adenium obesum
Height/Breadth: 10–16 inches/
10 inches (25–40 cm/25 cm)
Blooming Season: spring and fall
Fantastic stemmed succulent

▶ **long blooming**

Blooms: depending on type, white, red, or pink, with one or two colors; **Location:** sunny and warm (at least 68°F/20°C) all year; **Watering:** keep substrate moist from spring to fall (use thumb test), but avoid water-logging; **Fertilizing:** fertilize lightly every two weeks in the summer; **Care:** in spring, repot as needed in a shallow pot that's not too large, using loose soil; **Arrangement:** very effective as single plant or in shallow containers with other succulents that likewise don't root deeply.

Ornamental Pepper
Capiscum annuum
Height/Breadth: 10–12 inches/
8 inches (25–30 cm/20 cm)
Blooming Season: starting in June
Decorative annual plant

▶ **conspicuous-colored fruits**

Blooms: white, inconspicuous; the attractive fruits appear from early summer into winter in various shades of violet, red, and orange to yellow; **Location:** sunny to bright, but cool rather than too warm (not above 68°F/20°C); may spend the summer on a terrace in a sheltered location; **Watering:** keep moderately moist (water as needed; use thumb test); **Fertilizing:** every two weeks; **Care:** avoid drafts; **Arrangement:** very effective as single plants in small windows.

Flaming Katy
Kalanchoe blossfeldiana hybrids
Height/Breadth: 10 inches/6–8 inches
(25 cm/15–20 cm)
Blooming Season: year-round
Blooming annual plant

▶ **thick, waxy leaves**

Blooms: large flower heads in dark yellow, orange, red, and pink, in light and dark shades; **Location:** sunny (however, protect from direct midday sun), warm, and well ventilated; can also be placed in bright locations other than a sunny windowsill; **Watering:** water only when top soil is dry (use thumb test); **Fertilizing:** fertilize every two to three weeks; **Care:** air out thoroughly two to three times per day; **Arrangement:** attractive decoration for table and window; frequently planted with other plants in same container; also available in dwarf varieties.

EXPERT ADVICE
This plant's milky sap is poison-ous and irritating to skin.

EXPERT ADVICE
Leaf louse or spider mite infestations can occur if plant is kept too dry.

GOOD PARTNERS
Ivy, Creeping Fig, Ferns

Even though sunny, warm locations are appropriate for only a few houseplants, you can still have plenty of colorful blooming plants.

Light Green Kalanchoe
Kalanchoe miniata
Height/Breadth: 8–10 inches/up to 20 inches (20–25 cm/50 cm)
Blooming Season: February to March
Succulent flowering plant

▶ **distinctive bell-shaped flowers**

Blooms: bell-shaped, salmon-colored, apricot-colored, red, orange; **Location:** sunny to bright and warm; air out occasionally; in summer on the deck in a partially shaded location sheltered from the wind; **Watering:** water only as needed (use thumb test); leaves fall off when conditions are too moist; **Fertilizing:** during blooming fertilize every two to three weeks; **Care:** easy to propagate in soil with cuttings of tops or leaves; **Arrangement:** *K. Manginii* makes a fine hanging plant.

Regal Pelargonium
Pelargonium grandiflorum hybrids
Height/Breadth: 16 inches/10 inches (40 cm/25 cm)
Blooming Season: April to June
Bushy flowering plant

▶ **large flower heads**

Blooms: purple, pink or white, often with attractive darker markings, arranged in flower heads next to one another; **Location:** sunny, well ventilated and warm (around 68°F/20°C); cool during winter (around 59°F/15°C); **Watering:** water abundantly as needed (use thumb test), but avoid waterlogging; **Fertilizing:** fertilize once a week while blooming; **Care:** cut back about 2 inches (5 cm) in spring; repot every two years; easy to propagate with top cuttings in fall; **Arrangement:** interesting individual plant for windowsills.

Pentas
Pentas lanceolata
Height/Breadth: 12 inches/12 inches (30 cm/30 cm)
Blooming Season: September to January
Compact flowering plant

▶ **spherical-shaped plant**

Blooms: small, individual blooms in spherical flower heads in pink, salmon, and carmine; **Location:** in summer and fall, warm, bright, and well ventilated; in winter, cooler (around 59°F/15°C), sheltered from direct midday sun; **Watering:** use water at room temperature (after thumb test)—however, avoid both waterlogging and dried-out root ball; **Fertilizing:** give some fertilizer about every two weeks in summer; **Care:** after blooming, carefully cut back, repot, and cut back on water and fertilizer for a short while; **Arrangement:** attractive table decoration in winter.

EXPERT ADVICE
Becomes sparse with time; therefore take cuttings every year.

EXPERT ADVICE
Too much warmth in winter interferes with bud production.

EXPERT ADVICE
Even plants that like warmth appreciate a brief airing out of the room.

Decorative Leafy Plants

Urn Plant
Aechmea fasciata
Height/Breadth: 16–20 inches/
16 inches (40–50 cm/40 cm)
Blooming Season: July to September
Epiphytic leafy plant

▶ **large funnel-shaped bromeliad**

Blooms: noticeable blooms with pink
bracts and purple blooms; **Location:**
warm and sunny all year (above 65°F/
18°C); also tolerates warm air from
central heating; **Watering:** water
sparingly in leaf funnel every one to
two weeks in summer; in winter, every
three to four weeks; **Fertilizing:**
fertilize sparingly every two weeks in
summer; **Care:** mist on hot, dry days;
repot every two years; cut off and pot
runners after blooming, since the main
plant dies after blooming; **Arrangement:** good with other plants in
hydroponics.

Ponytail Palm
Beaucarnea recurvata
Height/Breadth: 3 feet/24 inches
(1 m/60 cm)
Blooming Season: doesn't bloom in
cultivation
Exotic indoor tree

▶ **an extraordinary plant**

Location: in summer, preferably in a
sunny spot on the deck sheltered from
rain; indoors, in a well-ventilated location; in winter, bright and cool; **Watering:** keep moderately damp (use
thumb test); very sensitive to excessive moisture; **Fertilizing:** fertilize
sparingly every two weeks in summer;
Care: repot every three years, covering
drainage hole with plenty of clay
shards; **Arrangement:** the amusing
shape makes it well suited to a spot
all to itself in the window.

Rosary Vine/String-of-Hearts
Ceropegia woodii
Length: 1–2 yards/meters
Blooming Season: year-round
Hanging plant

▶ **tropical creeping plant**

Blooms: interestingly shaped, pink-
colored tubiform blooms; **Location:**
sunny and warm year-round; however,
like a cooler spot in the winter;
Watering: better too little than too
much (use thumb test); **Fertilizing:**
fertilize sparingly in summer; **Care:**
repot every two to three years; at
that time, use long-term fertilizer;
Arrangement: hanging plant for a
window; can also be trained to grow
on a trellis.

EXPERT ADVICE
Increases in beauty with age

EXPERT ADVICE
*To propagate, let the nodules in
the leaf axils take root.*

It seem hard to believe, but there are even a few leafy plants that can tolerate lots of sun and heat, thanks to their special survival strategies.

Coleus

Coleus blumei hybrids
Height/Breadth: 16 to 20 inches/ 12 inches (40–50 cm/30 cm)
Blooming Season: summer
Leafy annual plant

▶ **beautifully marked leaves**

Blooms: light blue, fairly inconspicuous; **Location:** bright and sunny, but a little cool (no forced hot air; normal room temperature), sheltered from direct midday sun; **Watering:** water abundantly in summer, less in winter; keep from drying out; **Fertilizing:** fertilize every two weeks except in winter; **Care:** after a couple of months, plants become sparse; then put top cuttings into water; cut back young plants fairly often to encourage bushy growth; **Arrangement:** good background for yellow or orange flowering plants.

Ornamental Banana

Musa acuminata
Height/Breadth: 3 feet/4.5 feet (1 m/1.5 m)
Blooming Season: rarely blooms in cultivation
Attractive potted plant

▶ **fast-growing leafy plant**

Blooms: older plants produce impressive blooms; **Location:** in summer, preferably sunny and protected from the wind outdoors; in winter, bright and cool (approx. 61°F/16°C); **Watering:** water generously in summer (use thumb test), but sparingly in winter; **Fertilizing:** fertilize well weekly in summer; **Care:** repot in rich soil every two to three years; **Arrangement:** keep in large clay pot; in summer, put creeping and blooming plants around edge of pot.

Spineless Yucca

Yucca elephantipes
Height/Breadth: 12 to 24 feet/3 to 5 feet (4–8 m/1–1.5 m)
Blooming Season: rarely blooms in cultivation
Robust indoor tree

▶ **very popular houseplant**

Blooms: numerous, impressive, white to cream-colored, bell-shaped flowers; **Location:** preferably outdoors in summer; in winter, as bright and well ventilated as possible, and very cool (41–50°F/5–10°C); **Watering:** keep moderately moist; somewhat drier in cool winter quarters; **Fertilizing:** fertilize lightly every two weeks in summer; **Care:** repot every two to three years in the spring; place plenty of clay shards over the drainage hole, provide organic long-term fertilizer; use potting soil for flowers; **Arrangement:** tall, attractive individual plant for large rooms.

GOOD PARTNER
Yellow or orange blooming Flaming Katy

EXPERT ADVICE
Many nurseries have facilities for winter storage of plants.

EXPERT ADVICE
Plants that have grown too large can be sawed off and allowed to produce new shoots.

Container Plants for a Winter Garden

Blooming Plants for Sunny Locations

Plant	Bloom Color	Blooming Season
Agapanthus *Agapanthus praecox*	bluish purple	summer
Anisodontea capensis *Anisodontea capensis*	deep pink	early summer through fall
Strawberry Tree *Arbutus unedo*	white, cream-colored, pink	winter
Bougainvillea *Bougainvillea glabra*	red, purple, pink, orange, yellow, white	spring through late summer
Bird of Paradise Bush *Caesalpinia giliesii*	yellowish red	summer
Senna *Cassia corymbosa*	deep yellow	summer through early fall
Cestrum *Cestrum* varieties	white, yellow, pink, red	spring through fall
Broom *Cytisus x racemosus*	yellow	spring through early summer
Datura/Angel's Trumpet *Datura* varieties	white, yellow, cream-colored, pink, red, blue	early summer through fall
Coral Tree *Erythrina crista-galli*	red	summer through fall
Jacobinia *Jacobinia pauciflora*	yellowish red	winter
Crape Myrtle *Lagerstroemia indica*	deep pink	summer through late fall
Manuka *Leptospermum scoparium*	pink, white, red	winter through early summer
Mandevilla *Mandevilla laxa*	white, yellow, pink, purple	early summer through summer
New Zealand Christmas Bush *Metrosideros excelsa*	red	early summer
Myrtle *Myrtus communis*	white to cream-colored	early summer through fall
Oleander *Nerium oleander*	red, pink, cream-colored	summer
Scented Geranium *Pelargonium* varieties	white, pink, purple	summer

American Agave
Agave americana
Height/Breadth: 3 feet/4½ feet (1 m/1.5 m)
Blooming Season: only when older
Succulent rosette plant

▶ **thorny leaves**

Leaves: green or variegated; **Location:** full sun or outdoors in summer; bright and very cool winter quarters (just above freezing); **Watering:** water moderately (use thumb test), but keep fairly dry; **Fertilizing:** add fertilizer to water two to three times in summer; **Care:** repot younger plants every three years, taking care to assure good drainage; easy to propagate through offshoots; **Arrangement:** green and yellow specimens are particularly beautiful; Agave plants reach out quite far and are best set out in a "desert patch" in the winter garden.

Mediterranean Fan Palm
Chamaerops humilis
Height/Breadth: up to 4½ feet/up to 3½ feet (1.5 m/1.2 m)
Blooming Season: rarely blooms in cultivation
Bushy fan-shaped palm

▶ **bushy palm**

Blooms: paniculate blooms with yellowish individual flowers; **Location:** bright to sunny and well ventilated year-round; best outdoors in the summer, and somewhat cooler in the winter (approx. 61°F/16°C); **Watering:** water generously in summer months; the higher the temperature, the more water is needed; water sparingly in winter, leaving rather dry; avoid excess moisture at all costs; **Fertilizing:** fertilize sparingly every 14 days; **Care:** repot every two to three years; **Arrangement:** best used as individual plant in exposed locations.

EXPERT ADVICE
"Blunt" the long thorns on the ends of the leaves by sticking on a piece of cork.

EXPERT ADVICE
Careful: the stalks have sharp thorns.

Because of their size, some sun-loving plants are appropriate for the winter garden and for the deck or porch in the summer.

Coconut Palm
Cocos nucifera
Height/Breadth: up to 16 feet/up to 6 feet (5 m/2 m)
Blooming Season: rarely blooms in cultivation
Slow-growing pinnated palm

▶ **leaves initially nonpinnated**

Blooms: panicles of blooms with light yellow individual flowers; **Location:** as sunny and bright as possible, and warm and well ventilated year-round; **Watering:** always keep moderately moist (use thumb test); better dry than too moist; **Fertilizing:** fertilize once a month in summer months; **Care:** mist regularly with lime-free, lukewarm water to provide high humidity; in cultivation these trees don't grow to be very old; **Arrangement:** attractive plants that thrive best alone.

Common Fig
Ficus carica
Height/Breadth: up to 10 feet/up to 10 feet (3 m/3 m)
Blooming Season: spring or fall
Summer green bush

▶ **available in many varieties**

Blooms: small and inconspicuous; the multicolored, edible fruits of different shapes are rather appealing; **Location:** sunny and warm in the summer, bright and cool in the winter, and well ventilated year-round; **Watering:** water abundantly in the summer, but take care to leave no excess water; in winter merely keep the root ball from drying out completely; **Fertilizing:** fertilize sparingly once a week in the summer; **Care:** in spring, repot as needed in good, loose soil; **Arrangement:** large-growing plant that needs lots of space.

Canary Island Date Palm
Phoenix canariensis
Height/Breadth: up to 13 feet/up to 16 feet (4 m/5 m)
Blooming Season: rarely blooms in cultivation
Single-stemmed pinnated palm

▶ **very common type of cultivated palm**

Blooms: large clusters of blooms with yellow to cream-colored individual flowers; **Location:** sunny and warm in the summer, bright and cool in the winter, always well ventilated; **Watering:** water abundantly in summer, but sparingly in winter; never let root ball dry out; **Fertilizing:** fertilize every two weeks in the summer; **Care:** mist occasionally in the summer; in the spring, repot in good, loose soil as needed; trim around root balls that have become too large; **Arrangement:** best suited to standing alone.

EXPERT ADVICE
Coconut palms are usually sold in shops as sprouts.

EXPERT ADVICE
Some varieties produce fruit even without pollination.

CROSS REFERENCE
Caring for palms, page 57

Guests from Desert and Savanna

Aloe

Aloë variegata
Height/Breadth: 3 feet/28 inches
(1 m/70 cm)
Blooming Season: January–February
Leafy succulent

▶ **rosette-shaped succulent**

Blooms: long, erect, yellowish-orange
blooms; **Location:** prefers a warm,
sunny spot year-round, but can be
kept somewhat cooler in the winter; in
summer, can also spend time on a
sunny deck sheltered from wind and
rain; **Watering:** water sparingly; better
kept fairly dry; **Fertilizing:** feed a little
cactus fertilizer from time to time in
the summer; **Care:** repot every three
to four years in cactus soil or good,
loose substrate; **Arrangement:** best
kept singly.

Crown of Thorns

Euphorbia milii
Height/Breadth: 12–20 inches/
8–12 inches (30–50 cm/20–30 cm)
Blooming Season: October to June
Succulent flowering plant

▶ **an extraordinary plant**

Blooms: originally only red, but now
available in white, yellow, pink, red,
and purple; **Location:** warm and sunny
in summer, but bright and cool
(approx. 59°F/15°C) in winter to encourage blooming; hybrids can be
kept in a warm spot year-round;
Watering: keep moderately moist (use
thumb test), but don't let dry out;
Fertilizing: fertilize sparingly during
blooming season; **Care:** repot every
three to four years; **Arrangement:**
colorful, easy-to-care-for complement
in hydropots.

Living Stones

Lithops varieties
Height/Breadth: 2 to 2$\frac{1}{2}$ inches/
2$\frac{1}{2}$ to 3 inches (5–6 cm/6–8 cm)
Blooming Season: September to
October
Flowering succulent

▶ **stonelike leafy succulent**

Blooms: white and yellow; **Location:**
sunny, warm, and well ventilated; cool
from November to April (41–46°F/
5–8°C); hybrids should be kept warm
year-round; **Watering:** water only occasionally in saucer, or water the pot
every couple of weeks; avoid watering
between leaves; **Fertilizing:** fertilize
sparingly in the summer months;
Care: repot using new cactus soil
every three years; **Arrangement:** cover
substrate with sand or light gravel;
this tiny plant is also very attractive in
a small terrarium with other desert
plants.

EXPERT ADVICE
*Aloë arborescens grows in the shape
of a tree.*

EXPERT ADVICE
*The Euphorbia lomii hybrids are more
compact and have larger leaves.*

GOOD PARTNER
Small cactuses

These charming, often strange plants are almost indestructible. That makes them ideal for beginners.

Ponytail Palm/Elephant Foot Tree

Pachypodium varieties
Height/Breadth: 20 inches/16 inches (50 cm/40 cm)
Succulent leafy plant

▶ **palmlike stalk**

Blooms: in its natural setting, produces beautiful blooms; **Location:** warm and sunny year-round; **Watering:** keep moderately moist in winter; water very sparingly in summer (rest period); **Fertilizing:** fertilize sparingly in winter and early spring; **Care:** repot every four to five years in cactus soil; **Arrangement:** does well as a single plant on a sunny deck sheltered from the wind.

Sansevieria/Snake Plant/Mother-in-Law's Tongue

Sansevieria trifasciata
Height/Breadth: up to 3 feet/8 to 20 inches (up to 1 m/20–50 cm)
Blooming Season: spring
Succulent leafy plant

▶ **forms thick leaf clusters**

Blooms: older plants produce greenish-white, pleasant-scented blooms; **Location:** bright and warm (not below 59°F/15°C) year-round; protect from intense midday sun; varieties with all green leaves also tolerate partial shade; **Watering:** water as needed, but keep fairly dry; **Fertilizing:** fertilize sparingly with cactus fertilizer in the summer months; **Care:** repot in cactus soil as needed, in a fairly shallow pot; cut off runners and pot separately; **Arrangement:** very attractive in combination with multicolored varieties.

Tillandsia

Tillandsia varieties
Height/Breadth: 6 to 8 inches /4 to 6 inches (15–20 cm/10–15 cm)
Blooming Season: rarely blooms in cultivation
Epiphyte

▶ **small, gray shimmering leaves**

Blooms: earlike clusters of blooms with pink to purple flowers; **Location:** full sun and well ventilated; **Watering:** mist once a day in the summer using lukewarm water (the plant takes in water through its leaves); once a week in the winter; **Fertilizing:** add a little fertilizer to the spray from time to time in the summer; **Care:** in the winter, can be kept even cooler and drier; **Arrangement:** good as a hanging plant; hang the plant from a string in the window.

EXPERT ADVICE
Very low-maintenance houseplant, but thorny and poisonous

EXPERT ADVICE
Put plenty of clay shards over drainage hole when you repot.

EXPERT ADVICE
Buy only plants that are tied up to a stake.

Cactuses: Bizarre and Abundant Bloomers

Cactuses with Beautiful Blooms

Name	Bloom Color	Blooming Season
Rat's Tail Cactus *Aporocactus flagelliformis*	pink, red	spring
Goat's Horn Cactus *Astrophytum capricorne*	yellow	summer
Echinofossulo-cactus/ Brain Cactus	yellow, blue-violet, white	spring
Powder Puff Cactus *Mammillaria*	yellow, red, violet, white	spring
Notocactus	yellow, pink, violet	spring, summer
Ball cactus *Notocactus haselbergii*	red, yellow	spring, summer
Rebutia	yellow, violet, red	spring
Popcorn Cactus *Rhipsalis*	yellow	winter
Night Blooming Cereus *Selenicereus grandiflorus*	brown-white	summer

Peculiarly Shaped Cactuses

Name	Shape
Old Man Cactus *Cephalocereus senilis*	column-shaped stem, thick and covered with long, white hairs
Peruvian Pear Cactus *Cereus peruvianus*	column-shaped, dark green stem with branching crown, raised ribs around aureole
Golden Barrel Cactus *Echinocactus ingens*	spherical stem with sturdy brownish thorns
Ferocactus acanthodes	spherical to short, columnar stem with long, whitish, pink, or light red quills
Spider Cactus *Gymnocalycium mihanovichii*	small, spherical, with red and yellow protuberances
Trichocereus spachianus	green, many-ribbed column with short, white spines

Golden Barrel Cactus

Echinocactus grusonii

Height/Breadth: 4$^1/_2$ feet /31 inches (1.5 m/80 cm)
Blooming Season: summer
Spherical cactus

▶ **well fortified and covered with spines**

Blooms: yellow, pink to violet; yellow or white spines; **Location:** warm and sunny in the summer (but no direct sun), cool (around 50°F/10°C) and bright; **Watering:** water generously in summer (use thumb test), sparingly in winter; **Fertilizing:** fertilize once or twice a month with cactus fertilizer in the spring and summer; **Care:** repot as needed in spring or summer; **Arrangement:** a fine container plant because of its size and shape.

Silver Torch Cactus

Cleistocactus straussii

Height/Breadth: up to 13 feet/1$^1/_2$ to 2$^1/_2$ inches (up to 4 m/3–6 m)
Blooming Season: spring
Column-shaped plant

▶ **thick, snow-white covering of hairs**

Blooms: small, wine red; **Location:** sunny, warm, and well ventilated in summer; in winter, bright and cool (41–50°F/5–10°C); **Watering:** keep from drying out in summer, water occasionally (set pot two/three into immersion bath); in winter keep nearly dry; use lime-free water; **Fertilizing:** fertilize once or twice a month in the spring and summer with cactus fertilizer; **Care:** repot as needed in the spring in good, loose substrate; larger plants need a support; **Arrangement:** larger specimens make good container plants.

EXPERT ADVICE
Cactuses respond better to an occasional immersion bath than to regular watering.

CROSS REFERENCE
Taking care of cactuses, page 56

**Cactuses don't require much care,
but because of their many strange shapes they have
their own attractiveness.**

Epiphyllum

Epiphyllum hybrids
Height/Breadth: about 36 inches/
20 inches (90 cm/50 cm)
Blooming Season: spring and summer
Edges of shoots are wavy

▶ **large, colorful blooms**

Blooms: yellow, orange, red, purple,
white, even flaming bicolor; some
varieties are scented; **Location:** very
bright and well ventilated year-round,
protected from direct sun; keep at
50°F (10°C) in winter; **Watering:** keep
moist in spring and summer; water
sparingly during rest period, but keep
from drying out; use lime-free water;
Fertilizing: fertilize with cactus food
every two weeks in spring and summer; **Care:** repot in the spring or after
blooming; **Arrangement:** use broad,
shallow pot; some varieties also make
good hanging plants.

Opuntia Cactus

Opuntia varieties
Height/Breadth: up to 15 feet/
9 feet (5 m/3 m)
Blooming Season: summer
Flat, disc-shaped shoots

▶ **good grower**

Blooms: yellow, orange, red, white;
Location: sunny and warm in spring
and summer, preferably outdoors in a
spot sheltered from wind and rain;
very cool in winter (43–47°F/6–8°C),
bright and well ventilated; **Watering:**
water generously without waterlogging when growth begins in the
spring, thereafter as needed (use
thumb test); keep fairly dry in winter;
Fertilizing: give cactus food once or
twice a month in spring and summer;
Care: repot as needed in spring;
Arrangement: these are favorite
container plants because of their size
and shape.

Thanksgiving Cactus

Rhipsalidopsis gaertneri
Height/Breadth: 10 to 12 inches/
20 inches (25–30 cm/50 cm)
Blooming Season: spring
Jointed, flat shoot

▶ **abundant blooms**

Blooms: dark red, pink; **Location:** very
bright, but without direct sun, well
ventilated; warm in spring and summer (43–50°F/6–10°C); **Watering:**
keep moist in spring and summer (use
thumb test; avoid waterlogging);
water sparingly in fall and winter;
Fertilizing: provide cactus food every
two weeks in spring and summer;
Care: makes a good hanging plant.

Bright Locations

There is a particularly large selection of plants for bright locations, since light is the most important source of energy for plant growth and blooming.

Most blooming and leafy plants thrive best in a bright location.

What constitutes a bright location? A gardening lexicon defines it this way: the light intensity in a bright location is at least 2000 lux.

What Are Some Bright Locations?
Most plant lovers find themselves asking which of the rooms in their house are sufficiently bright, and how to determine that without using a lux meter.

The ideal place for plants that like it bright without being sunny and hot is a window that faces east. But there are many other places in the house where plants that like bright conditions can thrive. Here are some hints for selecting a location:
▶ Does your house stand some distance away from other houses and large trees?
▶ Do you live "higher up," in other words, on the second floor or higher?
▶ Does your house have large windows?
▶ Does your house have white or light-colored walls and floors?

▶ Do you have curtains in your windows?
▶ Does the sun shine into your house for a couple of hours each day?

If you can answer one or more of these questions with "yes," then you have ideal conditions for most houseplants.

Difficult Decisions
A tremendous number and variety of leafy and blooming plants need a bright location without direct midday sun. Here are a few criteria you can use in choosing:
▶ Many plants that like bright locations need high humidity, and must therefore be misted regularly with lime-free water at room temperature; is this possible in the location you're considering?
▶ Plants grow and thrive very well in the ideal location; is there also enough room for the plant to spread out over a fairly long time?

Plants Everyone Knows...

Aphelandra/Zebra Plants
Aphelandra squarrosa
Height/Breadth: 16 inches/10 inches (40 cm/25 cm)
Blooming Season: June to October
Flowering annual plant

▶ **leaves with beautiful markings**

Blooms: yellow; **Location:** preferably in bright, warm place without direct sun, but may be located most other places because it is short-lived; **Watering:** as needed (use thumb test) with lime-free, room-temperature water; **Fertilizing:** fertilize every two weeks; **Care:** in a warm location, mist frequently with lime-free water at room temperature; **Arrangement:** attractive individual plant for window-sills; also well suited to sprucing up darker locations for short periods of time.

Blooming Begonia
Begonia elatior hybrids
Height/Breadth: 12 inches/10 inches (30 cm/25 cm)
Blooming Season: year-round
Flowering annual plant

▶ **rich blooming plant that makes a good gift**

Blooms: white, yellow, pink, red, orange, single or double; **Location:** bright (no midday sun) and warm (at least 66°F/18°C); **Watering:** regularly as needed (use thumb test) with lime-free water; **Fertilizing:** every two weeks; **Care:** avoid placing too close to other plants; mildew occurs quickly at high humidity; air out two to three times a day; **Arrangement:** luxuriant blooming colors on windowsill, bookshelf, or console.

Cyclamen
Cyclamen persicum
Height/Breadth: 14 inches/10 inches (35 cm/25 cm)
Blooming Season: August to April
Flowering annual plant

▶ **a favorite potted plant for many years**

Blooms: pink, white, purple, red, marbled, with smooth or frayed leaf edges; **Location:** preferably bright and cool (59°F/15°C); **Watering:** water as needed (use thumb test) in saucer or cachepot; **Fertilizing:** once a week; **Care:** regularly remove brown leaves and wilted parts (grab them from underneath and pull them back); don't place too close to other plants; provide fresh air; **Arrangement:** very attractive in different colored groups on windowsills or in dishes.

EXPERT ADVICE
It's best not to move the plant around.

EXPERT ADVICE
To avoid rot, never water directly onto nodule.

You can find these potted plants cheaply practically everywhere; they are plants that bloom abundantly but live for only a short while.

Poinsettia
Euphorbia pulcherrima
Height/Breadth: 18 to 20 inches/16 to 18 inches (45–50 cm/40–45 cm)
Blooming Season: October to January
Flowering annual plant

▶ **colorful upper leaves**

Blooms: Blooms themselves are small and unremarkable, but the upper leaves are colorful; red, light red, salmon pink, pink, creamy white; **Location:** bright and warm, protected from direct sun; **Watering:** keep root ball evenly moist, but avoid waterlogging; **Fertilizing:** only once or twice after purchase; **Care:** for cultivating, cut back significantly after blooming, repot, and keep fairly dry; to encourage blooming starting in October, keep in total darkness for twelve hours a day; **Arrangement:** attractive in groups.

Persian Violet
Exacum affine
Height/Breadth: 8 inches/6 to 8 inches (20 cm/15–20 cm)
Blooming Season: July to September
Flowering annual plant

▶ **blooms have a slight fragrance**

Blooms: white, light purple; **Location:** bright at room temperature, without excessively strong direct sunshine; **Watering:** water as needed; avoid letting it dry out; **Fertilizing:** sprinkle on long-lasting fertilizer once or twice, or add some flower fertilizer to water every two weeks; **Care:** remove faded blooms to encourage more flowering; **Arrangement:** attractive bushy plant for small windowsills, kitchen windows, and table decorations.

Primrose
Primula obconica
Height/Breadth: 10 inches/5 inches (25 cm/13 cm)
Blooming Season: year-round
Blooming annual plant

▶ **a favorite harbinger of spring**

Blooms: purple, light purple, white, orange; **Location:** bright but protected from intense midday sun, as cool as possible (46–50°F/8–10°C); **Watering:** as needed (use thumb test); avoid waterlogging; **Care:** cut off wilted stems as low as possible; **Arrangement:** for windowsills and table decorations, preferably in color-coordinated cachepots.

GOOD PARTNERS
Ivy, Soleirolia, Creeping Fig

EXPERT ADVICE
Leaves can be irritating to skin.

Cheerful Colors

Lipstick Plant
Aeschynanthus radicans
Length/Breadth: 20 inches/
14 to 16 inches
(50 cm/35–40 cm)
Blooming Season: June to August
Perennial leafy and flowering plant

▶ **blooming hanging plant**

Blooms: yellow-orange or shiny red, cylindrical blooms; **Location:** bright and warm all year (around 68°F/20°C); **Watering:** as needed (use thumb test) with room-temperature, lime-free water; **Fertilizing:** use fertilizer tablet in spring or long-lasting fertilizer at repotting (approximately every two years); **Care:** mist fairly often; to encourage blooming, it's helpful to keep the plant very cool (around 59°F/15°C) and dry for a month in winter; **Arrangement:** attractive hanging plant near a window.

Hibiscus
Hibiscus rosa sinensis
Height/Breadth: up to 9 feet/4$\frac{1}{2}$ to 6 feet (3 m/1$\frac{1}{2}$ to 2 m)
Blooming Season: March to October
Perennial bush

▶ **large, tropical-appearing blooms**

Blooms: pink, yellow, white, orange, carmine, double or single; **Location:** in a warm, sunny spot in summer (starting in June); sink pot into soil; bright and at around 65°F/18°C in winter; **Watering:** water generously in summer; in winter as needed (use thumb test); **Fertilizing:** once a week; **Care:** cut back significantly and repot in January or February; mist frequently if indoor air is dry; **Arrangement:** solitary plant on windowsill, with larger specimens in a winter garden.

Amaryllis
Hippeastrum hybrids
Height/Breadth: 24 to 28 inches/10 inches (60–70 cm/25 cm)
Blooming Season: January to April
Perennial bulb plant

▶ **large, funnel-shaped blooms**

Blooms: red, white, orange, pink, white and red; **Location:** bright and warm in blooming season; **Watering:** water generously in blooming season; **Fertilizing:** refrain from fertilizing during blooming season; **Care:** when leaves appear, water generously and fertilize once a week; after about four months, cease fertilizing and water sparingly; remove dried leaves, and during the winter, keep the plant dark and cool (approx. 61°F/16°C); after that, force it on a warm, bright windowsill; **Arrangement:** a real eye-catcher on windowsill and tabletop.

EXPERT ADVICE
Also available as upright growing plant

EXPERT ADVICE
Bloom formation is encouraged by a fairly cool and dry rest period.

EXPERT ADVICE
Be sure to provide good drainage by putting clay shards over the drainage hole.

Flowering houseplants come in many different types, so you should be able to find any colors you want.

Azalea
Rhododendron simsii hybrids
Height/Breadth: 10 inches/12 to 16 inches (25 cm/30–40 cm)
Blooming Season: December to May
Perennial flowering plant

▶ **available in several varieties**

Blooms: pink, red, pink and white, or red and white, single or double;
Location: bright and as cool as possible (down to 65°F/18°C) while blooming; in summer, preferably outdoors in partial shade; in winter quarters, very cool (41–50°F/5–10°C) and bright; **Watering:** water generously while blooming; never let root ball dry out; **Fertilizing:** give Azalea fertilizer every two weeks from the end of blooming through August; **Care:** after flower buds open, repot and keep fairly warm; **Arrangement:** very attractive in groups.

African Violet
Saintpaulia ionantha
Height/Breadth: 4 to 6 inches/ 8 to 10 inches (10–15 cm/ 20–25 cm)
Blooming Season: year-round
Flowering plant in a variety of forms

▶ **also available in dwarf forms**

Blooms: violet, white, pink, also two-colored; edges of petals either wavy or smooth; **Location:** bright to partially shaded and warm (68°F/20°C and above); protect from intense sun; **Watering:** keep root ball moderately moist (use thumb test); use lime-free, room-temperature water; avoid moistening leaves; **Fertilizing:** every one to two weeks; **Care:** easy to propagate with leaf cuttings; about twelve hours of daylight per day are required for formation of blooms; **Arrangement:** for windowsills, consoles, and table decorations.

Christmas Cactus
Schlumbergera hybrids
Height/Breadth: 10 to 30 inches/18 to 20 inches (25–30 cm/45–50 cm)
Blooming Season: November to January
Leafy succulent

▶ **an attractive hanging plant**

Blooms: scarlet red, orange, pink, violet; **Location:** bright, no direct sun, warm, even outdoors protected from rain in the summer; **Watering:** in summer, always keep root ball moist; use lime-free water; **Fertilizing:** every two weeks in the summer; **Care:** for bloom formation, needs little watering and a month or two of rest at about 50–59°F/10–15°C at the start of winter; **Arrangement:** because of its overhanging, jointed stems, this plant needs to be placed in an elevated spot or used as a hanging plant.

CROSS REFERENCE
For special plant care, see page 56.

EXPERT ADVICE
Very sensitive to moisture, cold, and direct sun

EXPERT ADVICE
Once buds for blooms appear, don't move the plant.

Short-lived Splendor

Chenille Plant
Acalypha hispida
Height/Breadth: 14 to 16 inches/14 inches (35–40 cm/35 cm)
Blooming Season: summer
Flowering annual plant

▶ **long, downy clusters of blooms**

Blooms: red, pink, white; **Location:** bright and warm year-round, no direct midday sun; high humidity; **Watering:** as needed with room-temperature, lime-free water; keep root ball from drying out; **Fertilizing:** every two weeks; **Care:** mist fairly often; remove wilted parts immediately; to continue growing plant, repot in nutrient-rich substrate in spring; cut back plants that have become sparse; **Arrangement:** well suited to windowsills; *A. hispaniolae* makes a very beautiful hanging plant.

Slipper Plant
Calceolaria hybrids
Height/Breadth: up to 8 inches/up to 12 inches (20 cm/30 cm)
Blooming Season: March to May
Short-lived flowering plant

▶ **usually dies after blooming**

Blooms: yellow, orange, brown and red striped, slipper-shaped, and puffy; **Location:** bright to partially shaded, warm, no intense sun; well ventilated; **Watering:** the warmer the location, the more water is needed; keep the root ball from drying out; **Fertilizing:** fertilize moderately once a week; **Care:** break off wilted blooms; this is a one-season plant; **Arrangement:** this short-lived plant is well suited to brightening up darker areas, as a table decoration, and for planting in flats.

Flame-of-the-Woods
Ixora coccinea
Height/Breadth: 10 to 12 inches/12 to 16 inches (25–30 cm/30–40 cm)
Blooming Season: April to August
Flowering annual plant

▶ **thick, inflorescent clusters of blooms**

Blooms: yellow, orange, or red; **Location:** warm (68–72°F/20–22°C), humid, and bright; **Watering:** as needed while blooming (use lime-free, room-temperature water), keep from drying out; **Fertilizing:** to keep the plant alive longer after blooming, cut back dramatically, place in a fairly cool location (around 64°F/18°C); water less, withhold fertilizer; don't let root ball become too cool; also mist frequently during rest period; repot in spring; **Arrangement:** decorative individual plant for windowsills.

EXPERT ADVICE
Acalypha wilkensiana hybrids have beautifully colored leaves.

EXPERT ADVICE
Look for proper budding when buying a plant.

EXPERT ADVICE
The plant needs relatively high humidity.

There are some very beautiful blooming potted plants that, because of their short life span, are good for adding color even to darker locations.

Butterfly Rose

Rosa chinensis
Height/Breadth: 12 inches/8 inches (30 cm/20 cm)
Blooming Season: June to September
Short-lived flowering plant

▶ **richly blooming miniature roses**

Blooms: white, yellow, red, pink, orange, in light and darker shades; **Location:** as bright as possible to sunny and well ventilated; outdoors in the summer, bright and cool in the winter; **Watering:** keep root ball uniformly moist; **Fertilizing:** while blooming, fertilize every two weeks; **Care:** to keep plant alive, cut back and repot in the spring; **Arrangement:** attractive color for pots and flats; also good as individual plant on windowsills or as table decoration.

Cineraria

Senecio cruentus hybrids
Height/Breadth: 12 to 16 inches/12 to 16 inches (30–40 cm/30–40 cm)
Blooming Season: spring
Short-lived flowering plant

▶ **numerous, large composite blooms**

Blooms: white, red, pink, violet, brown-violet, and two-colored; **Location:** bright, well ventilated, and not too warm (about 64°F/18°C); **Watering:** water abundantly; the warmer the location, the more water; **Fertilizing:** every two weeks; **Care:** provide high humidity; **Arrangement:** a fine plant for cool rooms, staircases, and hallways; very pretty color combinations are possible.

Streptocarpus

Streptocarpus hybrids
Height/Breadth: 10 to 12 inches/10 to 12 inches (25–30 cm/25–30 cm)
Blooming Season: May to September
Flowering annual plant

▶ **long-stemmed, funnel-shaped flowers**

Blooms: violet, eggplant, white, salmon, pink, red, blue, with striped throat; **Location:** bright to partially shaded; warm in summer (around 68°F/20°C), a little cooler in winter (about 59°F/15°C); **Watering:** as needed (use thumb test); avoid waterlogging; **Fertilizing:** every three weeks; **Care:** put in a fairly warm and bright place to encourage blooming in spring; propagate sparse plants using leaf cuttings; **Arrangement:** ideal complement for dark-leafed foliated plants.

EXPERT ADVICE
You can also buy dwarf Butterfly Roses.

EXPERT ADVICE
When buying a plant, choose one that is not yet in full bloom.

EXPERT ADVICE
There are varieties that produce small blooms, many blooms, and a single large bloom.

Carefree but Beautiful

Jade Plant
Crassula ovata
Height/Breadth: up to 3 feet/20 inches (1 m/50 cm)
Blooming Season: only as it grows older
Succulent foliage plant

▶ **becomes bushy as it grows older**

Blooms: small, whitish flower heads; **Location:** bright, but no direct sun in summer (also outdoors, protected from rain); bright and cool in winter; also tolerates room temperature year-round; **Watering:** as needed (use thumb test)—avoid waterlogging; **Fertilizing:** fertilize sparingly in summer, especially if leaves lighten in color; **Care:** repot as needed in good, loose soil; use stable container; **Arrangement:** fits well in "succulent window;" a decorative individual plant as it grows older.

Dragon Plant
Dracaena varieties
Height/Breadth: 18 inches to 6 feet/up to 3 feet (0.5 to 2 m/1 m)
Blooming Season: doesn't bloom in cultivation
Tropical leafy plant

▶ **available in numerous varieties**

Leaves: green, yellow-green, in bunches on fairly long stems; **Location:** for variegated types, bright; for green-leafed varieties, partially shaded, at least 64°F/18°C, well ventilated; **Watering:** as needed (use thumb test), avoid waterlogging at all costs; **Fertilizing:** put in fertilizer stick in spring, or fertilize every two weeks in summer; **Care:** repot every one to two years; easy to cut back; **Arrangement:** put tall plants onto floor, lower ones onto windowsills or console.

Fiddle Leaf Fig
Ficus lyrata
Height/Breadth: 6 to 9 feet/32 inches (2–3 m/80 cm)
Blooming Season: doesn't bloom in cultivation
Perennial leafy plant

▶ **the largest ficus variety**

Leaves: large, shiny, dark green; **Location:** bright, at room temperature year-round; **Watering:** as needed (use thumb test)—tolerates no waterlogging; **Fertilizing:** fertilize lightly every four weeks in spring and summer; **Care:** wash leaves off from time to time; repot every two to three years, then drain well (place clay shards over drainage hole) and provide with long-term fertilizer; **Arrangement:** decorative individual plant that needs lots of room.

EXPERT ADVICE
Becomes more attractive and bushy with age

EXPERT ADVICE
Variegated types need more light and warmth than green-leafed varieties.

For people who don't have much time, but who still want to have some decorative greenery, carefree leafy plants are the obvious choice.

Sword Fern/Wild Boston Fern

Nephrolepis exaltata
Height/Breadth: 20 inches/24 inches (50 cm/60 cm)
Blooming Season: not a blooming plant
Perennial foliage plant

▶ **available in several varieties**

Leaves: depending on variety, of varying length and feathered fronds; **Locations:** bright and well ventilated year-round, at approximately 68°F/20°C; **Watering:** keep root ball uniformly moist; avoid waterlogging; **Fertilizing:** add fertilizer pin in spring; **Care:** mist frequently with lime-free water; in summer occasionally set out in rain, or rinse off in the shower; repot every two to three years; **Arrangement:** attractive background for blooming houseplants in flats or on a windowsill.

Baby Panda Bamboo

Pogonatherum paniceum
Height/Breadth: 20 to 28 inches/up to about 48 inches (50–70 cm/1.2 m)
Blooming Season: rarely blooms in cultivation
Tropical sweet grass

▶ **gracile, hanging stalks**

Leaves: light green; **Location:** sunny, fairly humid and warm (68–77°F/20–25°C) year-round; **Watering:** water abundantly and keep from drying out; **Fertilizing:** once a week in summer; **Care:** mist frequently in the morning or afternoon (but will tolerate fairly dry air); repot every year in spring and provide with long-acting fertilizer; divide larger plants; **Arrangement:** place in an elevated spot because of overhanging stems.

Tradescantia

Tradescantia zebrina
Height/Breadth: 8 inches/10 inches (20 cm/25 cm)
Blooming Season: summer
Robust hanging plant

▶ **leaves striped with silvery white**

Blooms: small, white to reddish; **Location:** bright all year, no direct sun, at room temperature and cooler (up to about 64°C/15°C); **Watering:** as needed (use thumb test), with lime-free water; keep root ball from drying out; **Fertilizing:** every two weeks in spring and summer; **Care:** repot in summer, spread long-acting fertilizer; cut plant back aggressively to encourage bushy growth; **Arrangement:** attractive plant in flats and hanging pots.

Bold and Beautiful Leaves

Alocasia
Alocasia varieties
Height/Breadth: 52 inches/31 to 39 inches (1.5 m/0.8–1 m)
Blooming Season: doesn't bloom in cultivation
Tropical leafy plant

▶ **sophisticated leafy plant**

Leaves: large, long-stemmed, shield-shaped, with white veins; **Location:** bright to partial shade, warm (72–77°F/22–25°C), humid, and free of drafts; **Watering:** as needed (use thumb test); keep root ball from drying out; **Fertilizing:** give liquid fertilizer once a month; **Care:** mist frequently; keep cool for winter storage (at 61°F/18°C); repot in good, loose soil every one to two years; **Arrangement:** the beautiful coloration and shape of the leaves deserve display in a conspicuous place.

Pineapple
Ananas comosus
Height/Breadth: 20 to 28 inches/3 feet (50–70 cm/1 m)
Blooming Season: rarely blooms in cultivation
Bromeliad

▶ **various decorative types**

Blooms: with age, compact, reddish clusters of blooms; **Location:** bright and warm (at least 65°C/18°C); **Watering:** as needed (use thumb test) with lime-free, room-temperature water; keep root ball from drying out; **Fertilizing:** mist fairly often; repot every two to three years; the main plant dies after blooming; at that time separate and plant the offspring; **Arrangement:** a striking solitary plant.

Caladium
Caladium bicolor hybrids
Height/Breadth: 28 inches/24 to 28 inches (70 cm/60–70 cm)
Blooming Season: doesn't bloom in cultivation
Tropical tuberous plant

▶ **very attractive foliage plant**

Leaves: green and white, red, green, and white, green and red, marbled, translucent; **Location:** bright during growing season (but no intense sun), warm (about 72°C/22°C) and humid; **Watering:** water abundantly during growth season, but avoid waterlogging; **Fertilizing:** every two weeks during summer; **Care:** mist frequently; in the fall the leaves retract; keep tuber warm and dry for the winter; in spring, repot, keep bright, warm, and humid, and begin watering; **Arrangement:** combine different colored varieties.

EXPERT ADVICE
The plant needs high humidity year-round.

EXPERT ADVICE
A very beautiful leafy plant, but not an easy one to take care of

Flowering plants aren't the only ones that bring color into the house; there are also plenty of houseplants that are remarkable for the coloration and the patterns of their leaves.

Croton
Codiaeum variegatum
Height/Breadth: 28 inches/22 inches (70 cm/55 cm)
Blooming Season: rarely blooms in cultivation
Foliage plant with multicolored leaves

▶ **numerous varieties available**

Blooms: horizontal clusters of small, greenish-white spherical flowers; **Location:** bright, warm (at least 65°F/18°C) and humid year-round; avoid direct sun; **Watering:** as needed with lime-free, room-temperature water; keep root ball from drying out; **Fertilizing:** add fertilizer stake in spring or fertilize about every four weeks through fall; **Care:** mist fairly often; repot every two to three years; **Arrangement:** a good plant for hydroponics.

Ti Plant
Cordyline fruticosa
Height/Breadth: up to 9 feet/6 feet (3 m/2 m)
Blooming Season: only with age
Tropical leafy plant

▶ **club-shaped, thickened roots**

Leaves: depending on type, green and white, green and yellow, red and green, long-stemmed, spear-shaped; **Location:** bright year-round (no intense sunshine), warm (at least 65°F/18°C), and humid; **Watering:** keep uniformly moist year-round; avoid waterlogging; **Fertilizing:** fertilize every two weeks during growing season; **Care:** mist fairly frequently with lime-free, room-temperature water; repot as needed in spring; **Arrangement:** very attractive in combination with light green foliate plants with small leaves.

Striped Screw Pine
Pandanus veitchii
Height/Breadth: 6 feet/6 feet (2 m/2 m)
Blooming Season: doesn't bloom in cultivation
Tropical foliage plant

▶ **thorny leaf clusters**

Leaves: green and white striped, long, narrow, thorny; **Location:** sunny to bright (no intense midday sun), warm, humid; **Watering:** as needed (use thumb test); keep root ball from drying out; **Fertilizing:** weekly in summer; **Care:** repot younger plants yearly, older ones only when the root ball becomes completely bound; with age, the plant forms roots like stilts that eventually lift it out of the pot; **Arrangement:** decorative leafy plant for large hydropot.

EXPERT ADVICE
The splendid colors of the leaves are preserved only in bright locations.

EXPERT ADVICE
Pests will infest this plant if the air is too dry.

EXPERT ADVICE
As it grows older, this plant protrudes farther; watch out for the thorns!

Elegant and Beloved Plants

Attractive Blooming Plants

Name	Bloom Color	Blooming Season
Kangaroo Paw *Anigozanthos flavidus*	red	summer
Coralberry/Spiceberry *Ardisia crenata*	white	early summer
Bleeding Glory Flower *Clerodendrum thomsoniae*	white and red	spring and summer
Kaffir Lily *Clivia miniata*	orange-red	spring
Rothschild Lily *Gloriosa rothschildiana*	red-yellow	summer
Malaysian Orchid *Medinilla magnifica*	pink-red	spring to summer
African Blood Lily *Scadoxus multiflorus*	orange-red	summer
Strelitzia *Strelitzia reginae*	orange-purple	winter-spring

Attractive Foliage Plants

Name	Type	Leaves
Maidenhair Fern *Adiantum* varieties	bushy	feathery fans
Norfolk Island Pine *Araucaria heterophylla*	upright, with horizontal branches	needlelike, dark green
Arabian Coffee Tree *Coffea arabica*	bushy tree	shiny, dark green, slightly wavy
Monterey Cypress *Cupressus macrocarpa*	column-shaped	needlelike, light green
Leea *Leea amabilis*	bushy	feathery, dark red
Para Para *Pisonia umbellifera*	bushy	large, green-white
Oyster Plant/ Cradle Lily *Tradescantia spathacea*	rosettelike, geometrically arranged leaves	sword-shaped, yellow-green with red undersides

Fishtail Palm
Caryota mitis
Height/Breadth: 4^1/$_2$ feet/3 to 4^1/$_2$ feet (1.5 m/1–1.5 m)
Blooming Season: rarely blooms in cultivation
Doubly feathered palm

▶ **unusually shaped leaves**

Leaves: double feathered leaves that resemble a fish tail, dark green; **Location:** warm (about 68°F/20°C) and bright year-round, no direct mid-day sun, humid; **Watering:** as needed; the root ball should be slightly damp on top, but not wet; **Fertilizing:** every two weeks in summer; **Care:** mist fairly frequently to provide high humidity; repot in spring only if the root ball is bound; **Arrangement:** best set on the floor, like all plants that grow tall.

King Sago Palm
Cycas revoluta
Height/Breadth: 6 feet/9 feet (2 m/3 m)
Blooming Season: doesn't bloom in cultivation
Tropical leafy plant

▶ **slow growing**

Leaves: arranged in cross shape, dark green, deeply indented; **Location:** well ventilated, bright in summer, but not in direct sun outdoors; bright and cool (about 59°F/15°C) in winter; **Watering:** generously in summer, as needed in winter; **Fertilizing:** every two weeks in the summer; **Care:** mist frequently in summer; repot in spring if root ball becomes bound; **Arrangement:** provides a tropical ambiance on deck or in winter garden.

EXPERT ADVICE
Plant needs constant care; not a good choice for people who travel a lot.

GOOD PARTNERS
Oleander, Bougainvillea

These plants require a special place in the home, for they are a feast for the eyes in every way.

Umbrella Plant

Cyperus varieties
Height/Breadth: 4¹/₂ to 6 feet/32 inches (1.5–2 m/80 cm)
Blooming Season: spring
Marsh plant

▶ **charming grass**

Blooms: small, inconspicuous grass blooms; **Location:** bright or partially shaded, warm; somewhat cooler in winter (about 65°C/18°C); **Watering:** water *A. alternifolius* generously (water should stand in saucer); *C. albostriatus* merely needs continually moist root ball; **Fertilizing:** every two weeks in summer; **Care:** repot in spring and divide plants to maintain robust leafing; mist fairly often; **Arrangement:** combine several large varieties.

Weeping Fig, Benjamin Tree

Ficus benjamina
Height/Breadth: up to 16 feet/6 feet (5 m/2 m)
Blooming Season: doesn't bloom in cultivation
Perennial foliage plant

▶ **many varieties**

Leaves: green, white-green variegated, dark green–light green variegated; **Location:** bright (as much light as possible from several sides), room temperature year-round; **Watering:** as needed in summer; in winter, only when the upper surface of the root ball becomes dry; **Fertilizing:** add fertilizer stake in spring; **Care:** repot in spring if root ball becomes bound; mist leaves fairly frequently; **Arrangement:** needs adequate space to show to advantage.

Indoor Linden/House Lime

Sparmannia africana
Height/Breadth: 6 feet/3 feet (2 m/1 m)
Blooming Season: January to March
Perennial foliage and flowering plant

▶ **familiar freestanding plant**

Blooms: white, in flower heads; **Location:** cool (59–68°F/15–20°C), bright and well ventilated; preferably even cooler in winter (41–50°F/5–10°C); **Watering:** water generously (soil should always be moist), but avoid waterlogging; **Fertilizing:** fertilize weekly in spring and summer; two or three times in the winter with plenty of time in between; **Care:** repot younger plants in the spring; older plants only if the root ball is bound; can be cut back; **Arrangement:** very attractive indoor tree for large, bright rooms.

EXPERT ADVICE
Never let Umbrella Plant dry out; provide high humidity.

EXPERT ADVICE
Leaves will fall off if kept too cool, too dark, too dry, or exposed to draft.

Charming Climbing and Hanging Plants

Asparagus Fern
Asparagus varieties
Height/Breadth: 20 to 24 inches/24 to 28 inches (50–60 cm/60–70 cm)
Blooming Season: summer
Needle-shaped leaf clusters

▶ **lacy fronds**

Blooms: small, white; **Location:** bright to partially shaded, room temperature (protect from direct sun); a little cooler in winter, if possible; **Watering:** keep root ball from drying out; water more sparingly at lower temperatures; **Fertilizing:** use fertilizer stake, or fertilize every two weeks in summer; **Care:** repot in spring if root ball becomes bound; **Arrangement:** just like ferns, the various types of *Asparagus* provide a decorative background for blooming plants.

Columnea
Columnea hybrids
Length/Breadth: 24 inches/16 to 20 inches (60 cm/40–50 cm)
Blooming Season: usually in spring
Decorative hanging plant

▶ **many varieties**

Blooms: orange-red, yellow; **Location:** bright and partial shade, warm year-round; **Watering:** water generously during growing season; keep root ball from drying out; use lime-free water at room temperature; **Fertilizing:** provide high humidity and warm soil; repot every two years after blooming in good, loose substrate; **Arrangement:** very attractive hanging plant near windows.

Wax Plant
Hoya varieties
Length/Breadth: 6 feet/16 to 20 inches (2 m/40–50 cm)
Blooming Season: April to September
Climbing evergreen plant

▶ **very fragrant blooms**

Blooms: white (*H. bella*) or pink (*H. carnosa*) with red spot in the middle, in large flower heads; **Location:** warm, bright to sunny (but no direct midday sun) year-round; *H. carnosa* even cooler in winter (50–59°F/10–15°C); **Watering:** as needed (use thumb test); avoid waterlogging; **Fertilizing:** use fertilizer stake in spring; provide trellis; repot every two to three years; don't cut off blooms after blooming; **Arrangement:** a good climbing or hanging plant.

EXPERT ADVICE
Available in many varieties, many of which make good hanging plants

EXPERT ADVICE
C. hirta and C.x kewensis need about eight weeks of cool rest in winter.

EXPERT ADVICE
H. carnosa is more robust than H. bella; don't move during blooming.

Because of the way they grow, these plants need an elevated place, a hanging pot, or a trellis.

Jasmine
Jasminium officinale
Length/Breadth: up to 9 feet/10 inches (3 m/25 cm)
Blooming Season: June to September
Evergreen climbing plant

▶ **very fragrant blooms**

Blooms: white; **Location:** bright, but not in full sun, moderately warm and well ventilated; in summer on a deck, sheltered from rain and wind; **Watering:** as needed with lime-free, room-temperature water; **Fertilizing:** every two weeks in summer; **Care:** cool (around 50°F/10°C), bright winter quarters are needed to foster blooming; water less frequently in winter; repot in spring; needs support for climbing; **Arrangement:** combine with dark-leafed foliage climbers; by itself, it appears quite lacy.

Passion Flower
Passiflora caerulea
Length/Breadth: 9 to 12 feet/6 inches (3–4 m/15 cm)
Blooming Season: June to September
Flowering climbing plant

▶ **exceptional bloomer**

Blooms: white/blue, pink to purple; **Location:** bright to sunny all year, outdoors and protected from wind in summer; cool (approximately 50–59°F/10–15°C) and well ventilated in winter; **Water:** water abundantly in summer; in winter, keep root ball from drying out; **Fertilizing:** fertilize once a week in summer; **Care:** repot as needed in spring using good, loose soil; needs climbing aid; **Arrangement:** impressive climbing plant, especially at blooming time.

Stephanotis
Stephanotis floribunda
Length/Breadth: 4½ feet/8 to 10 inches (1.5 m/20–25 cm)
Blooming Season: June to September
Demanding climbing plant

▶ **very fragrant blooms**

Blooms: white, in large flower heads; **Location:** bright and well ventilated year-round; warm in spring and summer, cool in fall and winter (around 55°F/13°C); **Watering:** water generously in summer, but avoid waterlogging; in winter, keep root ball from drying out; **Fertilizing:** fertilize well every two weeks during growth season; **Care:** mist occasionally; repot every two to three years in the spring; with plants that are losing their leaves, cut shoots back dramatically; **Arrangement:** very attractive single plant during blooming season.

Orchids: Queens of Flowering Plants

Orchids for Indoor Cultivation

Name	Bloom Color	Blooming Season
Cattleyas		
Cattleya bowringiana	purple, yellow, dark red	October to November
Cattleya labiata	pink, violet, red, orange-red	October to November
Dendrobium Orchids		
Dendrobium nobile	white, purple-red	March to June
Dendrobium phalaenopsis	dark purple-red	August to December
Laelia Orchids		
Laelia anceps	pink, violet, yellow	December to February
Laelia purpurata	pink, cinnabar	May to June
Pansy Orchids		
Miltonia candida	spotted yellow-brown, white, violet	August to November
Miltonia spectabilis	white, purple	August
Odontoglossum/Tiger Orchids		
Odontoglossum bictoniense	pink, yellow-green-red-brown	September to October
Odontoglossum maculatum	yellow-brown	March to April
Butterfly Orchids		
Oncidium ornithorhynchum	pink	October to November
Oncidium splendidum	spotted yellow, red-brown	October to December
Lady Slipper Orchids		
Paphiopedilum callosum	green, red, red-brown	February to March
Paphiopedilum insigne	yellow, yellow-green with light brown stripes	November to March
Moth Orchids		
Phalaenopsis amabilis	striped white, yellow, red	October to February
Phalaenopsis stuartiana	white, red-brown, green	January to March

Cattleya
Cattleya varieties
Height/Breadth: varies according to type
Blooming Season: differs according to type
Epiphytic orchid

▶ **blooms for weeks at a time**

Blooms: up to 7 inches (18 cm); pink, lilac, yellow, yellow-green, red, multicolored, often veined; **Location:** bright to sunny, well ventilated, warm (72°F/22°C); cooler during rest (54–59°F/12–15°C); **Watering:** only when substrate is truly dry; **Fertilizing:** every four weeks with half-strength flower fertilizer; **Care:** provide rest, or plant will not produce flowers; repot every three years at start of root growth; **Arrangement:** place orchids in a wooden tub or on an epiphyte stem.

Cymbidium
Cymbidium varieties
Height/Breadth: varies according to type
Blooming Season: spring to summer
Ground-hugging orchid

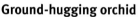

▶ **approximately fifty varieties**

Blooms: white, yellow, orange, pink, red, violet, brown, green, in a broad variety of mixtures; **Location:** well ventilated, bright, sunny, winter garden if possible (high daytime and low nighttime temperatures), 68°F/20°C in summer, nights 54–61°F/12–16°C; in winter 45–54°F/7–12°C, humid; **Watering:** as needed; keep substrate from drying out entirely; **Fertilizing:** give orchid fertilizer every four weeks; **Care:** repot if the substrate in the pot decomposes; **Arrangement:** attractive single plant.

EXPERT ADVICE
Whenever you buy an orchid, request specific information about how to care for it.

Orchids can't be beat for elegance, beauty, and color; unfortunately, most of them are very finicky houseplants.

Pansy Orchids
Miltonia varieties
Height/Breadth: varies according to type
Blooming Season: varies according to type
Epiphytic orchid

▶ **robust genus of orchid**

Blooms: yellow, pink, white, green, patterned; small- and large-flowered types and strains; **Location:** bright to partially shady, warm, no direct sun; high humidity; **Watering:** keep supplied with a regular amount of water; tolerates neither dry nor wet; **Fertilizing:** give orchid fertilizer with every watering; **Care:** cut stem off after blooming; repot if the substrate decomposes; don't spray plant directly; **Arrangement:** place in a wooden basket as a hanging plant or tie to tree trunk.

Lady Slipper
Paphiopedilum varieties
Height/Breadth: varies according to type
Blooming Season: varies according to type
Ground orchid

▶ **many varieties and strains**

Blooms: often yellow/green/dark red patterned; bloom for several weeks; **Location:** depending on variety, cool and bright or partially shaded and warm; request precise information about care when you purchase plant; **Watering:** water only when substrate is dry; don't water during rest period; **Fertilizing:** add orchid fertilizer to water only during growth phase; **Care:** repot once a year in potting soil for flowers; divide the plants only when they fall apart themselves; **Arrangement:** place in a wide plant container.

Moth Orchid
Phalaenopsis varieties
Height/Breadth: varies according to type
Blooming Season: varies according to type
Epiphytic orchid

▶ **numerous types and strains**

Blooms: white, pink, yellow, lilac, multicolored, patterned, brown-red, brown, green; **Location:** warm (70–77°F/22–25°C) during the day, 63°F/17°C at night; bright (no intense sun) and humid; a bit cooler during rest period; **Watering:** only when substrate is dry (use thumb test); don't water during rest period; **Fertilizing:** in growth season, add fertilizer to water; **Care:** repot every two years at start of growth season; leave two-thirds of stem after blooming; **Arrangement:** attractive in combination with ferns and bromeliads.

EXPERT ADVICE
Growth season is identifiable by new growth of roots and leaves

EXPERT ADVICE
Buy orchids only in a container and in bloom.

Partially

Shaded Locations

Even the places in your home where there's not much sunshine may be right for the pleasant green of houseplants.

People who have examined their homes critically to ascertain light conditions have probably concluded that not all rooms are flooded with ample sunshine and light throughout the day.

What's a partially shaded location?
Expressed in numbers, a partially shaded location is one where the light intensity is 1000 to 2000 lux.

When you consider that on a gray November day just 500 lux may reach a room, a partially shaded location is not necessarily dark, and often the transition from a bright to a partially shaded place is a fluid one.

Where are some partially shaded locations?
Bright to partially shaded rooms generally face north; they include bathrooms, kitchens, workrooms, and entryways.

If an apartment has large, undivided windows, is not surrounded by tall buildings or trees, or is on an upper story, then partial shade will be found where
▶ the sun shines into a room for only a few hours
▶ the plants are three to five feet (1–1.5 m) from a window;
▶ the light enters only indirectly (e.g., right under a window or next to a window)

If the apartment has smaller windows, is shaded (facing an inner courtyard with high trees or dark walls), or if it's on the lower floors, you can assume that all locations, except directly in a window, are shaded or partially shaded.

The Darker, the Cooler
Since most plants grow more slowly in partially shaded and shaded locations, you should take advantage of that and keep those places cooler, if possible.

You can even cut back on watering and fertilizing plants that are kept in darker places.

Most ferns thrive best in a partially shaded to bright, warm, and humid location.

Easy Care with Hydroponics

Flamingo Flower

Anthurium hybrids

Height/Breadth: up to 3 feet/2 to 3 feet (1 m/0.6–1 m)

Blooming Season: year-round

Perennial leafy and blooming plant

▶ **waxy, colored upper leaves**

Blooms: red, pink, white; **Location:** bright as well as partially shaded; avoid direct sun; warm (at least 68°F/20°C) and humid; **Watering:** as needed with lime-free, room-temperature water; plant tolerates no waterlogging; **Fertilizing:** about every four weeks in summer; **Care:** mist fairly often; repot in spring or summer if the plant starts to lift itself out of the pot; at that time shorten the root ball a bit; **Arrangement:** combine in large planters with other leafy plants.

Dieffenbachia

Dieffenbachia hybrids

Height/Breadth: 4½ feet/2 to 3 feet (1.5 m/0.8–1 m)

Blooming Season: doesn't bloom in cultivation

Tropical leafy plant

▶ **large, boldly variegated leaves**

Leaves: usually pronounced green and white or green spotted with yellow; **Location:** bright to partially shaded year-round, warm (around 68°F/20°C), and humid; **Watering:** as needed, preferably with lime-free water; **Fertilizing:** add fertilizer stake in spring, or fertilize every two weeks in summer; **Care:** mist fairly often; repot in spring if root ball becomes bound; **Arrangement:** most attractive in large planter with other leafy plants.

Taro Vine/Silver Vine

Epipremnum pinnatum

Length/Breadth: up to 16 feet/12 to 14 inches (5 m/30–35 cm)

Blooming Season: doesn't bloom in cultivation

Climbing or hanging plant

▶ **a favorite houseplant**

Leaves: shiny yellow-green; **Location:** bright to partly shaded year-round and warm (at least 60°F/16°C); **Watering:** as needed (use thumb test); **Fertilizing:** add fertilizer stick in spring, or fertilize every two weeks in summer; **Care:** the plant needs a climbing aid (wooden stake); otherwise it will hang down; repot every two years; **Arrangement:** climbing on a wooden stake, as ground cover in hydroponic plantings, or hanging down from furniture or shelves.

EXPERT ADVICE
A.-scheerzerianum hybrids should be kept cool (about 60°F/16°C).

EXPERT ADVICE
Varieties with lots of white or yellow need a bright location.

EXPERT ADVICE
Can also stay for several weeks in a shady spot

Sometimes people forget to water plants that are kept in workrooms or guest rooms; hydroponics can provide consistent living conditions.

Monstera/Swiss Cheese Plant
Monstera deliciosa
Height/Breadth: 16 feet/3 to 4 feet
(5 m/1–1.2 m)
Blooming Season: doesn't bloom in cultivation
Old, familiar foliage plant

▶ **deeply indented leaves**

Leaves: heart-shaped, dark green, variegated; **Location:** bright to shaded year-round, warm (approximately 68°F/20°C) and well ventilated; plants with variegated leaves need a bright location; **Watering:** as needed (use thumb test); **Fertilizing:** use fertilizer stick in spring, or fertilize from time to time year-round; **Care:** rinse the plant once or twice a year in the shower, or wipe off leaves with a damp cloth; provide strong climbing aid (wooden stake); **Arrangement:** ideal single and climbing plant for large rooms.

Philodendron
Philodendron varieties
Height/Breadth: various
Blooming Season: doesn't bloom in cultivation
Attractive leafy plant

▶ **many different varieties**

Leaves: vary in color and shape according to type of plant; **Location:** bright to partially shaded, warm (65–72°F/18–22°C); **Watering:** as needed (keep root ball slightly moist), avoid waterlogging; **Fertilizing:** every two weeks in summer; **Care:** always stake up plants; repot when root ball becomes bound; cut back as needed; **Arrangement:** well suited to hydroponic plantings in large rooms or offices.

Calla Lily/Lily of the Nile
Zantedeschia aethiopica
Height/Breadth: 32 inches/24 to 28 inches (80 cm/60–70 cm)
Blooming Season: January to June
A fine houseplant

▶ **elegant blooms**

Blooms: white, some strains also yellow, pink, and orange; **Location:** sunny to partially shaded, well ventilated; warm in summer (about 68°F/20°C); cool in winter (50–59°F/10–15°C); **Watering:** don't water for about eight weeks after blooming, then increase water a little; at start of and during blooming, water generously; **Fertilizing:** during budding and blooming, fertilize every two weeks; **Care:** repot as needed shortly before blooming; provide plenty of fresh air; **Arrangement:** looks best with dark-leafed foliated plants.

EXPERT ADVICE
Not suited to small rooms; it grows fast and needs lots of room.

GOOD PARTNERS
Philodendron, Monstera, Variegated Silver Vine

Large Leafy Plants for Partially Shaded Locations

Parlor Palm
Chamaedorea elegans
Height/Breadth: 3 feet/24 inches
(1 m/60 cm)
Blooming Season: summer
Widespread indoor palm

▶ **elegant palm in small format**

Blooms: branched, yellow panicles of blooms; **Location:** partially shaded and warm (about 68°F/20°C); also tolerates darker corners, but grows more slowly; **Watering:** as needed (use thumb test) with lime-free, room-temperature water; **Fertilizing:** add fertilizer stick in spring, or fertilize once a month in summer; **Care:** mist fairly often in heating season; repot every two to three years; cut off brown leaves or leaf tips with scissors; **Arrangement:** an attractive solitary plant for shelves and consoles.

Rubber Tree
Ficus elastica
Height/Breadth: 16 feet/3 feet
(5 m/1 m)
Blooming Season: doesn't bloom in cultivation
A familiar, old favorite

▶ **upright plant**

Leaves: large, dark green, and shiny, leathery and tough, also white and green variegated types; **Location:** bright (variegated types) or partially shaded and well ventilated, 61–72°F/16–22°C; **Watering:** as needed (use thumb test), avoid waterlogging; **Fertilizing:** add fertilizer stick in spring, or fertilize occasionally from spring through summer; **Care:** regularly wipe off leaves with a damp cloth; repot when root ball becomes totally bound; **Arrangement:** combine with small-leafed, bushy foliated plants.

Kentia Palm
Howeia forsteriana
Height/Breadth: up to 22 feet/13 feet
(7 m/4 m)
Blooming Season: rarely blooms in cultivation
A hardy type of palm

▶ **easy-to-care-for indoor palm**

Leaves: large, horizontal, dark green; **Location:** partially shaded year-round, warm (68–72°F/18–20°C) and well ventilated; in summer also outdoors in partial shade; **Watering:** keep root ball consistently moist; **Fertilizing:** every two weeks in summer; **Care:** mist fairly often in heated rooms; rinse the plant off in the shower once or twice a year or wipe off the leaves with a damp cloth; when root ball becomes totally bound, repot in spring; **Arrangement:** best by itself.

EXPERT ADVICE
Always use lime-free water at room temperature.

EXPERT ADVICE
Rubber trees grow tall very quickly.

CROSS REFERENCE
Caring for palms, page 57

Some large foliage plants do well with less light and provide plenty of indoor greenery.

China Doll
Radermachera sinica
Height/Breadth: up to 5 feet/up to 20 inches (1.5 m/50 cm)
Blooming Season: doesn't bloom in cultivation
Bushy foliage plant

▶ **grows quickly**

Leaves: double pinnated, shiny green; **Location:** bright to partially shaded, about 65°F/18°C; also outdoors in the summer, protected from rain and wind in a partially shaded spot; **Watering:** keep root ball uniformly moist; **Fertilizing:** every two weeks in spring and summer; **Care:** mist occasionally; repot young plants every year in the spring, older plants every three years; **Arrangement:** best by itself.

Dwarf Schefflera
Schefflera arboricola
Height/Breadth: 3 feet/51 inches (1 m/1.3 m)
Blooming Season: doesn't bloom in cultivation
Easygoing foliage plant

▶ **can lean out quite far**

Leaves: hand-shaped, dark green or variegated; **Location:** partially shaded in summer, room temperature and well ventilated; brighter and cooler (around 61°F/16°C) in winter; **Watering:** as needed (use thumb test) with lime-free water; **Fertilizing:** once a month in summer and fall; **Care:** mist fairly often if the plant is not well ventilated or is subjected to heating; wash off the leaves in the shower once or twice a year; provide good support (tie it up to a wooden or a fairly thick bamboo stake); **Arrangement:** an attractive solitary plant for large rooms.

Syngonium/Nephthytis/ Arrowhead Vine
Syngonium hybrids
Length/Breadth: up to 59 inches/24 to 28 inches (1.5 m/60–70 cm)
Blooming Season: doesn't bloom in cultivation
Tropical climbing plant

▶ **various strains**

Leaves: depending on kind of plant, green or variegated, arrowhead-shaped when young and with multiple lobes when older; **Location:** bright to partially shaded, warm (68°F/20°C and above), and humid; **Watering:** keep root ball as uniformly moist as possible (use thumb test); **Fertilizing:** every two weeks in summer; **Care:** mist fairly frequently, provide climbing aid; repot into a shallow pot in the spring when root ball becomes totally bound; **Arrangement:** an attractive hanging plant, or arrange in hydropot with other foliage plants.

EXPERT ADVICE
This plant needs adequate room to grow freely.

EXPERT ADVICE
Schefflera actinophylla and its strains are equally robust.

EXPERT ADVICE
Variegated types need a brighter location than green-leafed ones.

Plants for Shelves and Consoles

Maranta
Maranta leuconeura
Height/Breadth: 8 to 10 inches/18 inches (20–25 cm/45 cm)
Blooming Season: doesn't bloom in cultivation
Creeping plant

▶ **decorative leaf markings**

Leaves: delicate green with brown spots, velvety; **Location:** partially shaded, warm (65–68°F/18–20°C) and humid; **Watering:** keep root ball uniformly moist; keep from drying out, and use only lime-free water at room temperature; **Fertilizing:** once a month in spring and summer; **Care:** repot every one to two years; at that time provide long-acting fertilizer and polystyrene pellets to keep the soil loose; mist fairly frequently; **Arrangement:** looks best in an arrangement with dark green leafy plants.

Peperomia
Peperomia varieties
Height/Breadth: 8 inches/10 to 12 inches (20 cm/25–30 cm)
Blooming Season: some varieties bloom in summer
Epiphytic leafy plant

▶ **many different varieties**

Leaves: tough, wrinkled or fleshy, shaped and colored differently according to type; **Location:** partially shaded; rather warm (at least 65°F/18°C) for variegated types; **Watering:** as needed, when upper surface of root ball becomes dry; **Fertilizing:** once a month in summer; **Care:** mist fairly often; repot every two years in a shallow pot; **Arrangement:** combine different varieties in shallow planters; *P. caperata* produces small, club-shaped clusters of flowers.

Cretan Brake/Table Fern
Pteris cretica
Height/Breadth: 12 to 16 inches/16 to 20 inches (30–40 cm/40–50 cm)
Blooming Season: not a blooming plant
Not a long-lasting fern

▶ **comes in many varieties**

Leaves: several pinnated types of leaves, green and white-and-green variegated; **Location:** partially shaded to shaded, warm and temperate (61–68°F/16–20°C), humid; **Watering:** keep root ball uniformly moist; use lime-free water; **Care:** mist fairly often; avoid draft; repot every year or two and provide long-acting fertilizer; **Arrangement:** attractive in planters with blooming plants and ivy.

EXPERT ADVICE
Calathea, Ctenanthe, and Stromanthe are similar in appearance and requirements.

EXPERT ADVICE
Thick-leafed varieties will also tolerate dry air.

EXPERT ADVICE
Very well suited to a bottle garden

There are a number of perennial small-leafed foliage and blooming plants even for partially shaded locations on small pieces of furniture, shelves, and consoles.

Strawberry Begonia
Saxifraga stolonifera
Length/Breadth: 12 to 16 inches/6 to 8 inches (35–40 cm/15–20 cm)
Blooming Season: summer
Rosettelike hanging plant

▶ **forms plantlets on runners**

Blooms: white ridges; leaves dark green on top surfaces, violet underneath; "Tricolor" is green on topside with a white edge; **Location:** bright to partially shaded and rather cool (below 68°F/20°C); **Watering:** as needed (use thumb test); will not tolerate waterlogging; **Fertilizing:** provide fertilizer stick in spring, or fertilize once a week in spring and summer; **Care:** repot only when pot is fully root bound; **Arrangement:** very attractive hanging plant, especially when there are plenty of plantlets.

Soleirolia
Soleirolia soleirolii
Height/Breadth: 4 to 6 inches/10 inches (10–15 cm/25 cm)
Blooming Season: doesn't bloom in cultivation
Foliage plant that grows in a cushion shape

▶ **compact, spherical growth**

Leaves: small, light or dark green; **Location:** bright to partially shaded, well ventilated, and cool (not above 68°F/20°C); **Watering:** as needed (use thumb test), in saucer; tolerates no waterlogging or drying out of root ball; **Fertilizing:** feed long-acting fertilizer at repotting; **Care:** divide and repot each year to preserve compact growth; can also be cut back; **Arrangement:** unusual ground cover in planters or a nice single plant in a rustic clay pot on the windowsill.

Tradescantia
Tradescantia varieties
Length/Breadth: 20 inches/8 to 12 inches (50 cm/20–30 cm)
Blooming Season: summer
Parti-colored leafy hanging plant

▶ **striped leaves**

Blooms: small, white, or pink; **Location:** partially shaded, rather cool (59–68°F/15–20°C) and well ventilated; not sunny, otherwise the leaves will lose their color; **Watering:** as needed; keep root ball from drying out; **Fertilizing:** provide fertilizer stick in spring, or fertilize once a month in summer; **Care:** don't repot; it's better to cut the plants back significantly, or let four or five cuttings root in water and then pot them; **Arrangement:** attractive ground cover in large hydropots; unusual hanging plant.

EXPERT ADVICE
The many plantlets at the end of the long, red stems are very attractive.

EXPERT ADVICE
A location that's too warm produces excessive, spindly growth.

EXPERT ADVICE
Leaves are green or striped green, white, and pink.

Shady Locations

Some houseplants get by with a minimal amount of light. Like desert plants, they have developed strategies for surviving under extreme environmental conditions.

According to gardening lexicons, the light in shaded locations has an intensity of about 1000 lux—in other words, about a quarter of the intensity that's available in a spot right next to a window.

Where Are Some Shaded Locations?
We can find shaded locations where
▶ the sun doesn't shine into the room all day long (even in summer)
▶ a room and its windows look out on a dark backyard
▶ the plants are placed more than six feet (2 m) away from large windows
▶ the room has no windows
▶ the room absorbs lots of light because of dark or heavily patterned walls and/or floors, dark furniture, lots of objects in the room, and curtains in the windows.

Things to Look For
Many plants that thrive in and prefer a shaded location come from the tropical rain forest, where they live under the thick canopy provided by large trees.
▶ Plants that come from jungle regions do quite well in a fairly dark place in the summer; however, in the winter, when the days are shorter and more overcast, they should be placed in a brighter place for a couple of weeks.
▶ Plants that are normally kept in a bright place can also spend a short time in a darker spot. Plants that like shade, though, often tolerate poorly a sudden change from a shaded to a bright location. They should be acclimated gradually to the brighter location.
▶ The same applies when plants are placed outdoors in the summer.
▶ Plants that like shade simply can't tolerate intense sun. Their leaves burn in the truest sense of the word if they are exposed to the sun.

Depending on the season, short-lived blooming plants (such as Cineraria) can beautify shaded locations.

Robust Houseplants

Parlor Palm
Aspidastra elatior
Height/Breadth: 3 feet/31 to 36 inches (1 m/0.8–1 m)
Blooming Season: rarely blooms in cultivation
Robust leafy plant

▶ **forms thick tufts of leaves**

Leaves: shiny, dark green, tough; **Location:** shady to bright, no intense sun (61–68°F/16–20°C), and well ventilated; **Watering:** as needed (use thumb test); avoid waterlogging; **Fertilizing:** add a fertilizer stick in the spring, or fertilize every week or two in the summer; **Care:** provide fresh air circulation; wipe off the leaves fairly frequently with a moist cloth; repot when plant becomes root bound (in spring or summer); at that time it's also possible to divide the rhizome; **Arrangement:** this plant needs an elevated spot because its leaves hang down.

Bird's Nest Fern
Asplenium nidus
Height/Breadth: 20 to 24 inches/24 to 28 inches (50–60 cm/60–70 cm)
Blooming Season: not a flowering plant
Epiphytic fern

▶ **funnel-shaped leaf rosette**

Leaves: light green, shiny, non-pinnated; **Location:** shaded to partial shade, warm (about 68°F/20°C), well ventilated; **Watering:** as needed, preferably with lime-free water; **Fertilizing:** addition of long-acting fertilizer at time of repotting is adequate; **Care:** mist fairly frequently; repot every two to three years when the plant becomes root bound; the ball should be kept warm, so in drafty places a polystyrene or cork coaster should be placed under the plant; **Arrangement:** an attractive plant for the bathroom.

Dragon Tree
Dracaena marginata
Height/Breadth: 4½ feet/24 inches (1.5 m/60 cm)
Blooming Season: doesn't bloom in cultivation
Robust dracaena

▶ **palmlike foliation**

Leaves: dark green with a red border; **Location:** shaded to partially shaded; room temperature or a little cooler (to about 59°F/15°C); **Watering:** as needed; avoid waterlogging; **Fertilizing:** provide with long-acting fertilizer in spring; **Care:** repot when the plant is root bound; **Arrangement:** a handsome solitary plant for corners or next to the sofa.

EXPERT ADVICE
Varieties with green-and-white striped leaves need more light.

EXPERT ADVICE
Rapid scale insect infestation in light, dry locations

EXPERT ADVICE
All other Dracaena varieties need a bright location.

Even though these plants are robust, you can't neglect them; they still need some care to thrive and grow.

Fatshedera
x Fatshedera lizei
Height/Breadth: 3 feet/20 inches (1 m/50 cm)
Blooming Season: doesn't bloom in cultivation
Cross between Ivy and Aralia

▶ **also yellow parti-colored varieties**

Leaves: leathery, tough, hand-shaped, lobed, dark green; **Location:** shaded to bright, rather cool and well ventilated; in winter very cool (about 50°F/10°C); **Watering:** as needed; keep root ball from drying out; **Fertilizing:** every two weeks in spring and summer; **Care:** air out frequently if kept in a warm room, and mist from time to time; repot young plants yearly, older ones every two to three years; plants can be cut back at repotting to encourage bushy growth; **Arrangement:** handsome background for blooming plants in planters.

Japanese Aralia/Fatsia
Fatsia japonica
Height/Breadth: up to 6 feet/36 to 59 inches (2 m/1–1.5 m)
Blooming Season: rarely blooms in cultivation
Well-known leafy plant

▶ **grows quickly**

Leaves: large, hand-shaped, shiny, dark green; **Location:** shaded to bright, but not sunny; well ventilated and cool (61–68°F/16–20°C in summer, 43–50°F/6–10°C in winter); **Watering:** always keep root ball slightly moist; in winter, water a bit less; **Fertilizing:** every two weeks from spring through fall; **Care:** repot in spring if plant is totally root bound; cease cutting back plant as it grows older; **Arrangement:** solitary plant that needs lots of room; can be placed in a shaded place on deck or terrace in summer.

Spathiphyllum/Peace Lily
Spathiphyllum varieties
Height/Breadth: up to 3 feet/20 to 32 inches (1 m/50–80 cm)
Blooming Season: March through September
Herbaceous flowering plant

▶ **elegant blooms**

Blooms: white, green-white; **Location:** shady to bright, no intense sun, warm (65–68°F/18–20°C); humid air; **Watering:** always keep root ball slightly moist from spring through fall; avoid waterlogging, but keep root ball from drying out; water less in winter; **Fertilizing:** every four weeks from spring to fall; **Care:** mist frequently; repot in spring if root bound; **Arrangement:** favorite plant for large hydroponics plantings.

Climbing and Hanging Plants that Like Shade

Cissus
Cissus varieties
Length/Breadth: up to 16 feet/16 to 28 inches (5 m/40–70 cm)
Blooming Season: doesn't bloom in cultivation
Precocious creeping plant

▶ **climbing or hanging plant**

Leaves: Kangaroo Vine (*C. antarctica*) has downy, notched leaves, and Grape/Oak Leaf Ivy (*C. rhombifolia*) has shiny, rhomboidal or pinnated leaves ("Ellen Danica"); **Location:** partially shaded to shaded and not too warm (61–68°F/16–20°C); **Watering:** only as needed (absolutely no waterlogging); use water at room temperature; **Fertilizing:** every two weeks in spring and summer; **Care:** provide climbing aids for vertical growth; repot every two to three years; can be cut back; **Arrangement:** very effective room divider.

Spider Plant
Chlorophytum comosum
Length/Breadth: 3 feet/24 inches (1 m/60 cm)
Blooming Season: spring and summer
Fast-growing hanging plant

▶ **3-foot-long flower stems**

Blooms: small, white, and long, bow-shaped stems; **Location:** shaded to bright, no special temperature requirements; **Watering:** as needed; root ball should be kept from drying out; **Fertilizing:** use fertilizer stick in spring, or fertilize every two weeks in summer; **Care:** repot when roots push out of pot; the numerous stolons are easy to root in water; **Arrangement:** handsome but domineering hanging plant that needs lots of room.

Creeping Fig
Ficus pumila
Length/Breadth: 20 inches/8 inches (50 cm/20 cm)
Blooming Season: doesn't bloom in cultivation
Robust Ficus variety

▶ **striking hanging plant**

Leaves: rounded, heart-shaped, dark green; variegated types are also available; **Location:** bright to shaded, rather cool (61–68°F/16–20°C) and well ventilated; **Watering:** as needed; avoid waterlogging; **Fertilizing:** occasionally in spring and summer, or use a fertilizer stick in spring; **Care:** repot in spring if root bound; for vertical growth, tie up to stake; **Arrangement:** a favorite for planters, as a hanging plant, or ground cover.

EXPERT ADVICE
When conditions are too cool, too wet, or too dark, leaves turn brown and fall off.

EXPERT ADVICE
A good plant for beginners

EXPERT ADVICE
Variegated types need a brighter, slightly warmer location.

Even staircases and hallways, shelves in a room, and room dividers can be brightened up with luxuriant foliage plants.

Ivy
Hedera varieties
Length/Breadth: 3 feet/8 to 16 inches (1 m/20–40 cm)
Blooming Season: rarely blooms in cultivation
Robust climbing plant

▶ **many varieties**

Leaves: a great variety of shapes and colors; **Location:** bright to shaded for green-leafed types; bright to partially shaded for variegated types; fairly cool year-round (about 61–68°F/ 16–20°C) and well ventilated; **Watering:** as needed (use thumb test); **Fertilizing:** use fertilizer stick in spring, or fertilize every two to four weeks in summer; **Care:** repot in spring if root bound; **Arrangement:** favorite climber and ground cover in small and medium planters.

Heartleaf Philodendron/ Parlor Ivy/Cordatum Vine
Philodendron scandens
Length/Breadth: 15 feet/24 inches (5 m/60 cm)
Blooming Season: doesn't bloom in cultivation
Tropical climbing plant

▶ **very robust**

Leaves: green, very variable in size and shape; **Location:** bright to shaded; preferably at room temperature (about 68°F/20°C); **Watering:** as needed; avoid waterlogging; **Fertilizing:** use fertilizer stick in spring; **Care:** mist fairly frequently if plant is kept in heated, dry room; provide climbing aids; repot every two to three years; **Arrangement:** attractive ground cover in hydropot, and as a hanging or climbing plant.

Staghorn Fern
Platycerium bifurcatum
Height/Breadth: 8 inches/up to 3 feet (20 cm/1 m)
Blossoming Season: not a blooming plant
Epiphytic fern

▶ **leaves shaped like antlers**

Leaves: two different types: antler-shaped leaves and recessed leaves that shroud the root ball; **Location:** partially shaded to shaded, warm (about 65°F/18°C) and humid; **Watering:** keep uniformly moist by immersing pot once a week for about a half hour or by watering between the recessed leaves; **Fertilizing:** add a little fertilizer to the water from time to time in the summer; **Care:** mist fairly frequently; **Arrangement:** best in a stable hanging pot.

GOOD PARTNERS
Flaming Katy, Parlor Palm, Garden Primrose

EXPERT ADVICE
Robust and easy to care for, good for mediocre locations

EXPERT ADVICE
Draws its nutrients from rotted leaves

Plant Arrangements

Beautifying Your

Home with Plants

You can buy houseplants in the widest range of colors, shapes, and sizes, so there are no limits to the arrangements that are possible.

One thing's for sure: foliage and flowering plants make for a more pleasant atmosphere and beautify every room. So why not play a little with the many shapes and colors that are available?

Plants in Arrangements

The great selection of houseplants on the market offers an amazing array of possibilities for beautifying the home:
▶ Flowering plants bring color into the home.
▶ Creeping, fast-growing plants are great choices for green room dividers and for hiding unattractive surfaces.
▶ Large, elegant solitary plants (known as solitaries or specimen plants) can serve as eye-catchers in large rooms.
▶ Small, multicolored or unusual potted plants, in conjunction with all types of attractive accessories, constitute small works of art on windowsills, tables, and consoles.
▶ Indoor fountains, planters, hanging plants, and columns of plant growth are exceptional elements in arrangements.
▶ Dwarf varieties provide table decorations year-round and make it unnecessary to buy expensive flower arrangements.

Incorporating Accessories

Some simple accessories make it possible to decorate with delightful plant arrangements. Here are a couple of suggestions:
▶ Mussel shells, dried starfish, and snail shells go well with plants in a bathroom or guest bath.
▶ Sand and gravel are good substrate covers for cactuses and succulents.
▶ Forsythia and willow branches are a must for spring bloomers in dishes or glass containers.
▶ Pumpkins, colored leaves, dried pinecones, and rose-hip twigs serve to accent fall arrangements.
▶ Tree roots and pieces of bark complement tropical plants and ferns, especially in plant terrariums.

People who have discovered the joy of houseplants will continue to acquire more of them.

Varied Colors and Shapes

Houseplants can be divided into two groups: flowering and foliage or green plants.

▶ Flowering houseplants are effective mainly through their multicolored blooms, which appear at various times throughout the year, depending on variety, and which can be combined with one another in the greatest number of ways.

▶ Green or foliage plants rarely or never bloom in cultivation. They captivate with their many leaf colors and shapes.

Plants with Different Shapes

Each plant has its own distinctive shape that is determined by the size of the plant, the number of its stems, stalks, or branches, and the arrangement and size of its leaves.

Based on their shape, houseplants can be roughly divided into the following groups:

▶ plants that grow upright with straight or overhanging growth (such as Dieffenbachia, Dragon Tree, Fatshedera, Rubber Tree, and Ti Plant)

▶ bushy plants such as Cyclamen, Coleus, Poinsettia, and Japanese Aralia

▶ climbing plants such as Cissus, Stephanotis, Passion Flower, and Wax Plant

▶ pendant or trailing plants such as Ivy, Scindapsus, Hanging Philodendron, and Zebrina

▶ pulvinated or cushion-shaped plants such as Soleirolia

▶ rosette plants such as Urn Plant, Bird's Nest Fern, and African Violet

Plants that have peculiar shapes include Ponytail Palm and many cactuses and succulents.

What Shape Is Right for Which Place?

For a plant to look its best, it needs to be placed in the right spot. Here are a few tips:

▶ Place small plants at eye level or slightly lower.

▶ Rosette plants should always be viewed from above.

▶ Large, upright growing varieties should be placed on the floor, small plants such as Fiddle Leaf Fig next to higher pieces of furniture (such as cupboards and consoles), and massive plants such as Split Leaf Philodendron by large pieces of furniture.

With larger plants, it's a good idea to first measure how much space they will need, figuring in growth, for they may eventually take up as much room as a large piece of furniture.

▶ Let climbing plants grow near a shelf or a small cupboard; you'll have to provide climbing aids such as wire or a stake.

▶ Hanging or pendant plants are as effective as climbing plants for dividing rooms.

▶ Pulvinated plants are very effective as an underlayer in large pots and planters.

A Circle of Color

One way to combine colors successfully is a circle that represents the whole color spectrum.

How Colors Work

Colors have a wide variety of effects on people:

▶ White and cream colors come across as cool, discreet, and soothing.

▶ Yellow and orange provide a feeling of warmth and cheer people up.

▶ Red and pink exude warmth, but they shouldn't be too obvious, for they are naturally a little overpowering.

▶ The so-called "cool" colors, blue and green, have a calming effect.

Combination of reds: Amaryllis, Azaleas, Elatior Begonias, and Flaming Katy.

Color Combinations

Using the color spectrum, it's possible to create beautiful, peaceful color gradations, various shadings, and totally disparate color combinations.

▶ A peaceful, harmonious atmosphere comes from colors that lie next to one another on the color wheel, such as yellow and orange. Caution is advised for combinations of pink and red or blue and green; the colors can clash if they collide too forcefully with each other.

▶ Combinations of colors that are opposite one another on the color wheel—the complementary colors—can appear lively and friendly; examples are blue and orange, and red and green.

What Always Works

▶ Color combinations in uniformly warm or cool shades

▶ A single type of flowering plant in various colors and sizes

▶ White variegated foliage plants and white flowers

▶ Plants of the same color but different shapes, such as the light green of Bull Rush with the light green of Bird's Nest Fern.

▶ Large- and small-bloomed plants of a similar flower color

▶ Multicolored, variegated ground plants and blooming plants that echo one of the colors

Accessories for Every Taste

Overview

Accessories for the Bath

cachepots that match the color of the tiles

mussel shells, snail shells, starfish, and other items from the beach

glass items that match the colors of towels and bath mats

ceramic fish

Accessories for the Kitchen

soup tureens

baskets

baking tins as cachepots

metal baskets for hanging plants

colored tin cans for kitchen herbs

artificial fruits and vegetables for color accent

Accessories for Windowsills

clay or porcelain animal figurines

glass marbles in various colors

colorful wooden figurines to put into flowerpots

candles

The Right Cachepot

Your personal taste is the most important factor in choosing the color and shape of a cachepot. In any case, the cachepot should be large enough so that it's a little taller than the regular pot and allows about a finger's breadth of space around it. The proportions between plant height and pot should be on the order of 1:1 for small, low plants; for somewhat larger, usually annual flowering plants, 2:1; and for taller plants and solitaries, 3:1.

Pots for Solitary and Container Plants

Large solitary plants, container plants, cactuses, and succulents are best kept in clay pots and planters; these come in warm shades of yellow, orange, red, and brown.

Containers come in the broadest range of sizes and shapes, plain, decorated, or with relief designs, untreated or glazed. Untreated containers need a waterproof saucer underneath.

The right accessories are much more than decorative additions. They show plants off to best advantage and accentuate a style of living.

Hanging Plants: Fine Additions

There are many types of pots and decorative cachepots for hanging plants. Be sure to choose a pot with enough room at the top so that when you water it doesn't run over the edge. The cachepot must be waterproof to keep water from dripping onto the floor. Be sure that the pot is very secure, for damp soil is heavy, and your plant will gain in mass and weight every year. Watering cans with long spouts are the best choice for watering elevated plants.

Plant Etageres and Flower Benches

Flower benches and plant etageres are a good choice if you have no more room on windowsills and floors to accommodate your plants. An etagere can hold several plants on several levels. A flower bench is a little lower and usually has one or two levels.

You can get both plant holders in wood, plastic, or metal, and it's worth it to invest in a handsome one, since it will remain a focal point in the room for a long time.

Creating Prominent Eye-Catchers

Various accessories placed among green and blooming plants lend a personal note to an arrangement and help set up a focal point.

Flowering plant arrangements can be rounded out with objects that accentuate colors, such as glass balls, figurines, colored stones, and candles.

CROSS REFERENCE
Charming Climbing and Hanging Plants
pages 100–101

Playing with Colors

Overview

White Blooming Houseplants

Cyclamen, Azalea,
Spathiphyllum/Peace Lily,
Flamingo Flower, Hyacinth,
Jasmine, Wax Plant, Calla Lily

Yellow Blooming Houseplants

Flowering Begonia, Flaming
Katy, Aphelandra/Zebra Plant,
Narcissus, Slipper Plant

Orange Blooming Houseplants

Flowering Begonia, Clivia,
Flaming Katy, Ixora/Flame-of-
the-Woods, Lipstick Plant

Red and Pink Blooming Houseplants

Cyclamen, Amaryllis, Azalea,
Primrose, Flowering Begonia,
Hibiscus, Hyacinth, Ixora/
Flame-of-the-Woods, Chenille
Plant, Penta, Butterfly Rose,
Poinsettia

Blue Flowering Houseplants

Primrose, Persian Violet, Streptocarpus, Campanula/Clustered
Bell Flower, African Violet

All in White

White in combination with various
shades of green looks noble and
elegant.

Some masterful combinations
include Spathiphyllum (*Spathiphyllum
floribundum*), Lorraine Begonia, the
white blooming type of Persian
Violet (*Exacum affine*), Wax Plant
(*Stephanotis floribunda*), and the
white variegated type of Weeping Fig
(*Ficus benjamina*). But white is not for
everybody; when you give flowering
plants as a gift, you should remember
to find out the recipient's favorite
color.

Mixing Shades

To keep mixed shades of plants from
becoming boring, you should add
some leafy plants with light green,
filigreed leaves, or a white blooming
variety. In this planter, light blue
primrose (*Primula oboconica*), blue
hyacinths, and garden primrose
are broken up with white Jasmine
(*Jasminum officinale*) and small-
leafed, white variegated Ivy.

> **EXPERT ADVICE**
> *When you combine different types of*
> *plants, be sure their needs are similar.*

Thanks to the great number of types and strains available in the marketplace, you have a broad selection to choose from.

Light, Warm Hues

You can always create a dominant focal point in a room or on a window-sill with red, yellow, and orange flowering plants (in this case, Flaming Katy *Kalanchoë blossfeldiana* and Amaryllis in combination with Asparagus Fern *Asparagus densiflorus*).

Setting up Contrasts

If you place colors together that are opposite each other on the color wheel, you automatically create a strong contrast, as in this case with yellow and blue primroses.

There's Always Room for Green

You can combine any favorite flower color with the light green hues of leafy plants such as Piggyback Plant (*Tolmiea menziesii*) (here combined with Gerbera, Guzmania, and Elatior), Maidenhair Fern, Bird's Nest Fern, Bull Rush, Soleirolia, Asparagus Fern, Bamboo, Creeping Fig, and light variegated Ivy. You simply have to arrange the various large plants so that the tallest ones are toward the rear and the shortest toward the front.

Color Triads

You can create a color triad by drawing a triangle on the color wheel and choosing the colors that correspond to the three points.

Our example shows a combination of red (Gerbera), blue (*Campanula*/Clustered Bell Flower), and yellow (Flaming Katy), Chrysanthemum, and Abutilon/Parlor Maple that are complemented by a white-red *Miltonia* orchid hybrid.

CROSS REFERENCE
Color wheel, page 122

EXPERT ADVICE
Another color triad is a combination of green, orange, and violet.

Choosing the Right Plants

Overview

Slender, Upright Plants

Snake Plant, Dragon Plant, Fiddle Leaf Fig, Rubber Plant, Silver Spear, Yucca, Norfolk Island Pine

Broad, Upright Plants

Philodendron, Parlor Palm, Peace Lily, Kentia Palm, Coconut Palm, Japanese Aralia

Small Plants

Cyclamen, Cineraria, Azalea, Flowering Begonia, Flaming Katy, Clustered Bell Flower, Butterfly Rose, African Violet

Climbing and Hanging Plants

Philodendron, Ivy, Silver Vine, Swiss Cheese Plant, Spider Plant, Hanging Philodendron, Youth on Age/Piggyback Plant, Chenille Plant, Grape Ivy, Columnea, Wax Flower, Passion Flower, Syngonium, Kangaroo Vine, Lipstick Plant, Wax Plant, Tradescantia, Zebrina, Asparagus Fern, Jasmine

Long-Stemmed Eye-Catcher

A blooming long stem or a Weeping Fig with a twisted stem is a real joy indoors. Many houseplants are offered for sale as long stems, or can be grown as such; examples are Hibiscus (see photo), Azaleas, citrus trees, and Weeping Fig.

Relaxed Room Dividers

Climbing or trailing plants are very well suited for use as green room dividers. Plants that have small or light-colored leaves (Asparagus Fern/*Asparagus asparagoides* and Sword Fern/*Nephrolepsis* in the photo) create a light and playful effect; plants with large or dark leaves are more imposing.

You can achieve some remarkable effects in your home by using the many types of houseplants.

Luxuriant Veils

In contrast to climbing plants, hanging plants usually reach out a good deal farther and are more luxuriant in their growth, as the pictured Sword Fern (*Nephrolepsis exaltata* "Linda") shows.

Hanging plants are well suited for large windows and brightly lighted areas of a room. They are ideal for offices, since they liven up the room with their friendly green without taking up workspace.

Bonsais

Bonsais (*Ficus benjamina* "Starlight" in the photo) are little works of art that should be presented as such; in other words, at eye level, by themselves, and without distractions.

In addition to the Weeping Fig, the following houseplants are also available in bonsai form: Azalea, various types of *Ficus,* Umbrella Tree (*Schefflera arbolicola*), various succulents, and citrus trees.

Small Flowering Plants

Arranged in planters or in trays, small flowering plants make very attractive decorations for consoles and tables. Here is an elegant arrangement of red Butterfly Roses in white pots.

Small-Format Green Plants

Small-format green plants are gaining in popularity; the photo shows red mini-Begonias, Youth on Age, and Button Fern.

If you want to enjoy the green plants for a longer time, they should be transplanted to a larger pot or a terrarium so that the root ball doesn't dry out so quickly.

EXPERT ADVICE
Hang the pots in such a way that you can water them easily.

EXPERT ADVICE
When you buy a bonsai, ask where you can get it cut back.

A Variety of Decorative Leafy Plants

Overview

Plants with Variegated Leaves

Alocasia, Creeping Fig, Snake Plant, Coleus, Dieffenbachia, Dragon Plant, Ivy, Silver Vine, Swiss Cheese Plant, Spider Plant, Strawberry Begonia, Climbing Fig, Croton, Maranta, Table Fern, Schefflera, Screw Pine, Tradescantia, Wax Plant, Zebrina, and Peperomia

Plants with Grasslike Leaves

Baby Panda Bamboo, Umbrella Plant

Palms

Parlor Palm, Date Palm, Fishtail Palm, Kentia Palm, Coconut Palm, and Mediterranean Fan Palm

Ferns

Maidenhair Fern, Staghorn Fern, Bird's Nest Fern, Table Fern, Sword Fern

Playing with Leaf Shapes

Green plants are effective in many ways: by their shape and size, different leaf colorings and structures, and various leaf shapes. This tremendous variability makes possible a broad range of combinations. The various leaf shapes play a major role in this plant arrangement involving Alocasia/*Alocasia amazonica*, Pony Tail Palm (*Beaucarnea recurvata*), and Peace Lily (*Spathiphyllum*).

Indoor Trees

If there is enough space and light available, large green plants create a cozy atmosphere that can be further emphasized by choosing decorative cachepots.

From left to right: Malabar Chestnut (*Pachira aquatica*), Yucca (*Yucca elephantipes*), Australian Ivy (*Muehlenbeckia adpressa*), *Citrus mitis* "Variegata," Weeping Fig (*Ficus benjamina,* complemented by *Ficus pumila*), and Dragon Plant (*Dracaena marginata*).

EXPERT ADVICE
Mist plants with multicolored leaves fairly frequently and keep them in a bright location.

EXPERT ADVICE
Large plants that are kept in warm rooms need more frequent watering.

Foliage plants also lend themselves well to combinations. Take advantage of their rich variety of colors, shapes, and sizes.

Ferns for Warm, Humid Rooms

Ferns develop from thick, fleshy rhizome roots and simple or compound feathered or unfeathered leaves of varying length and width, depending on the type. Since the plants thrive best in warm, humid locations, they are best suited to adding greenery to a bathroom.

From left to right in the photo: Button Fern (*Pellaea rotundifolia*), Bird's Nest Fern (*Asplenium nidus*), and Peperomia (*Peperomia*).

Lacy Green

Grasses create an airy, light, and refreshing effect, as this arrangement of Baby Panda Bamboo (*Pogonatherum Paniceum* "Buxus"), Soft Rush (*Juncus spiralis*), and Umbrella Plant (*Cyperus alternifolius*) clearly demonstrates.

Grasses lose quite a lot of water through transpiration, and thus make a significant contribution to the indoor climate. The root ball should therefore always be kept moist.

Umbrella Plant likes humid places, especially when it's kept on a plant saucer that's continually filled with water.

A Breath of the Exotic

Palms always create a rather tropical atmosphere, especially when they are combined with other appropriate plants:

with Banana (*Ensete* or *Musa*) in a bright, cool location, House Lime (*Sparmannia africana*), and Azaleas; with Dragon Plant, *Ficus* varieties, and Philodendron in bright, warm rooms; at higher humidity also with orchids, bromeliads, and ferns. Photo: Chinese Fan Palm (*Livistona chinensis*), Begonias, and Streptocarpus (*Streptocarpus wendlandii*).

EXPERT ADVICE
Mist ferns fairly often with lime-free room-temperature water.

EXPERT ADVICE
Grasses need to be kept in a fairly bright location.

EXPERT ADVICE
Choose a fairly plain cachepot for large palms.

Arrangement Ideas

Water in a room livens things up, but it also increases humidity.

Any home can be beautified with houseplants, whether they are displayed singly or grouped or planted together.

Smaller, less conspicuous individual plants may get lost in a room. They benefit from being placed or planted with a group of other plants.

Planters

Foliage and flowering plants that are combined with others in a planter or some other fairly large plant container often show up better and are more interesting than if they were in individual pots spread around the room. The possibilities for combinations planted together are restricted to plants that have the same needs for light, temperature, food, and water.

Groupings of Plants

In contrast to individual plants that are planted together to form groups, specimens in separate pots that are placed together need only the same light and temperature conditions. Since each plant in this case has its own pot, it can be watered and fertilized individually.

A Few Ground Rules

▶ No plants should be overshadowed by larger, taller, or broader ones. Arrange the plants in large steps according to size.

▶ If the plant arrangement is easily visible from all sides, put the largest plants in the center and the others toward the outside in decreasing order of size. Place at the edge any creeping plants that hang over the sides of the container.

▶ If the container is against a wall, either arrange the plants in a triangle, i.e., large plants in the center and plants of decreasing size to the left and right, or place the large plants behind and smaller ones in front.

▶ Groups of plants that are set up next to a wall should fit in with the background in color and shape. Multi-colored blooms or leafy plants, or green plants with a wide variety of leaf shapes should be placed in front of a plain background.

Grouping and Combining Plants

Groups of plants become interesting when they combine various leaf shapes and structures, plants of the same or different colors, blooms of different sizes, and individual plants of different shapes and sizes.

Plant groups can
▶ liven up rooms, adding color and living green
▶ divide or unify rooms, or define limits
▶ disguise unattractive corners
▶ even out different heights, and
▶ bring the different seasons into the house

Plants as Room Dividers

Plants can be used quite easily and attractively in dividing large rooms into two or more areas. Depending on if the room is really to be divided or only subdivided optically, you can use plants on consoles, trellises or espaliers, tub planters, hanging and climbing plants in combinations or by themselves, or various sizes of plant groupings.
▶ You can create a loose, green wall with different small, leafy, climbing or creeping plants (such as variegated ivy, types of *Cissus*, Silver Vine, and Climbing Philodendron), which are either trained on an espalier or allowed to hang down, or with trailing plants (such as Spider Plant, Strawberry Begonia, Tradescantia, and Asparagus Fern) that are set on shelves at different heights.
▶ Several upright plants such as Dragon Plant, Rubber Plant, and Yucca in various sizes placed together and unified by identical cachepots can create a strong optical division.
▶ A plant container or fairly large urn filled with foliage and flowering plants can help define the atmosphere and the boundaries of sitting and eating places.

Plants on Windowsills

There is a very broad choice among plants appropriate for windowsills. One limitation is the width of the windowsill, so only small to medium plants are likely candidates.
▶ A kitchen window is a fine location for all types of herbs.

Livening Up Planters

Planters with seasonal flowering plants provide a bit of nature in the house.

▶ A sunny living room window is an ideal place for plants that crave the sun, such as cactuses and succulents, or imports from the Mediterranean and tropical regions.
▶ A window that looks out onto a backyard can be converted into a green and flowering indoor garden with the help of flower shelves installed in the window.
▶ A bright windowsill makes it possible to set up a fragrant window display or a tropical garden of ferns and orchids.

Seasonal Plant Groupings

Plant groupings that consist only of blooming plants, or of leafy and blooming plants, can reflect the seasons if flowering plants are included.
▶ Typical plants for winter include Cyclamen, Amaryllis, Cineraria, Azalea, Christmas Cactus, and Poinsettia.
▶ Primrose and bulb plants such as Crocus, Hyacinth, Narcissus, and Tulips appear in the spring.
▶ Summer offers a variety of flowering plants in the house as well as the garden; these include Barbeton Daisy, Clustered Bell Flower, Hortensia, Slipper Plant, and Butterfly Rose.
▶ In the fall, multicolored Chrysanthemums and heathers are the major contributors of color to plant arrangements.

Soleirolia, Wine Cup Primrose, Azalea, Sword Fern, and Ivy block the view of the backyard.

Arrangement Tips

There are no fixed rules for aesthetics with houseplants; combining and grouping plants is up to each person's taste.

But here are a few tips for people who may not be entirely sure of their tastes:

▶ Simple green leaves are good for showing off multicolored leafy plants to advantage.

▶ Green plants among flowering plants create a soothing effect.

▶ Tall plants among lower ones create tension in the grouping.

▶ Plant accessories and containers can unify plant groupings or distinguish between them.

▶ Trailing or climbing plants that hang over the edge of the pot are relaxing to people.

▶ Plants of different shapes contribute zest to a grouping.

▶ Variety among leaves is a source of color.

▶ Special plant furniture (shelves, tables, columns, and plant troughs) serve to keep plants together and provide adequate space.

Plants in Difficult Locations

Overview

Plants for Bright, Cool Rooms

Cyclamen, Amaryllis, Azaleas, Scented Geraniums, Hibiscus, Jasmine, Clivia, Wax Flower, and Parlor Maple

Plants for Dark Rooms

Philodendron, Silver Vine, Swiss Cheese Plant, Youth on Age, Kangaroo Vine, Schefflera, Parlor Palm, Japanese Aralia

Plants for Small Windowsills

Persian Violet, Soleirolia, Ivy, Creeping Fig, Tillandsia, Peperomia

Robust Plants for Dividing Rooms

Asparagus Fern, Philodendron, Ivy, Ivy Tree, Silver Vine, Swiss Cheese Plant, Spider Plant, Climbing Philodendron, Syngonium, Sword Fern

Adding Greenery to Staircases and Hallways

Staircases and hallways frequently don't offer many places for plants, and they usually are not well lighted. You can still add some pleasant greenery by choosing climbing and hanging plants that like shade.

You can attach a plant to a rope and pulley and hang it right by the light source, and simply lower it for watering (see illustration).

Subdividing Rooms

It's easy to divide a room by placing large plants in a group or in a row right on the floor and interrupting the view.

A more pronounced division is achieved by using a set of shelves filled with hanging and climbing plants such as Spider Plant, variegated Ivy, and Cissus.

CROSS REFERENCE
Plants for shaded locations, pages 114–117

CROSS REFERENCE
Shade-tolerant climbing and hanging plants, pages 116–117

Even difficult locations such as staircases and hallways can be made more appealing with plants.

Moving Large Plants Easily

Because of its light conditions, the spot in front of a door that opens onto a deck or terrace is a great one for many attractive, large house and container plants—except for the problem of opening and closing the door.

A simple solution to moving large plants easily involves plant rollers; large container plants are placed on these and easily pushed from one place to another. Garden centers offer plant rollers in various sizes, colors, and shapes.

Greening Up Dark Corners

Corners of rooms are often appropriate places to sit comfortably and read; but unfortunately, in the long run they are usually too dark for most houseplants—even the ones that tolerate shade and partial shade—especially in the overcast winter months.

Special plant lights can provide the necessary help in these cases. Gardening shops offer all kinds of lights that go with any decor.

Neutralizing an Unattractive View

The view out a window may be less than attractive. But there's a cure for that: convert your window into a plant shelf. To preserve the ease of opening the window, the shelves have to be attached right to the window frame (see illustration).

Plants that stand on the windowsill should be placed together in a fairly large container so you have just one container to move aside when you open the window.

A Place in the Sun

Overview

Sun-Loving Climbing Plants

Bougainvillea,
Passion Flower

Sun-Loving Hanging Plants

Rosary Vine, Light Green
Kalanchoe, Tillandsia

Sun-Loving Flowering Plants

Crown of Thorns, Regal
Pelargonium, Flaming Katy,
Cactuses, Pentas, Desert
Rose, Ornamental Pepper

Sun-Loving Green Plants

Pony Tail Palm, Urn Plant,
Ponytail Palm, Sansevieria,
Tillandsia, Yucca

Lots of Colors on the Windowsill

Windowsills that face south or south-west provide plenty of sun and are exceptionally sunny and warm locations, especially at midday in the summer, that are very appealing to succulent plants with tough or fleshy leaves and imports from Mediterranean and tropical regions.

You can arrange attractive window displays using a broad choice of plants for sunny locations, including hanging and climbing plants and low to medium green and flowering houseplants. (Left to right in picture: Bougainvillea, Orange Tree, Regal Pelargonium, Passion Flower; hanging plant: Rosary Vine)

Regardless of the plants you wish to combine, be sure that the plants aren't crowded together. The leaves of individual plants should be separated from one another by two to four inches (5–10 cm). Water in the morning or evening and only on the top of the root ball or in the saucer, since drops of water on the leaves of plants in sunny locations can quickly lead to burns.

CROSS REFERENCE
Plants for sunny locations,
pages 74–75

Charming representatives from the steppes and the deserts of the world are waiting to occupy a place in a sunny window.

A Taste of the Desert

Some typical denizens of hot and dry areas populate this windowsill (from left to right): Rat's Tail Cactus (*Aporocactus flagelliformis*), Golden Barrel Cactus (*Echinocactus grusonii*), Agave, Echeveria (*Echeveria*), Pony Tail Palm (*Pachypodium*), Crown of Thorns (*Euphorbia milii*), and String of Beads (*Senecio herreanus*).

People respond to these amusing plants, which have long thorns and fleshy leaves and stems, with reactions ranging from enthusiasm to indifference.

Flowering Sun Worshipers

For people who prefer flowers as eye-catchers in the window, here's a combination of easy-to-care-for Mamillaria with different colored flowers. The small globular cactuses are the best choice for the windowsill, and they delight every year with their luxuriant blooming in the summer months.

Planters for Warm Locations

This planter with Flaming Katy (*Kalanchoë blossfeldiana* hybrids), Thanksgiving Cactus (*Rhipsalidopsis* hybrids), and Rochea (*Crassula*) looks striking, and it's a great decoration for table or console in warm, sunny locations. None of these succulent plants is demanding or difficult to care for. They can easily be left to themselves for some time, since the thick, fleshy leaves store water.

EXPERT ADVICE
Plants with thorns and poisonous juices should be kept out of the reach of children.

CROSS REFERENCE
Cactuses: Bizarre and Abundant Bloomers, pages 84–85

Plants as Gifts

Overview

Gift Ideas for Minor Occasions

Dwarf varieties in appropriate cachepots

Shaped climbing plants

Small green plants in hydropots

Seasonal planters (spring-time greeting, Easter planter, fall plants, Advent or Christmas planter)

Kitchen herbs, individually or several together in appropriate planters

Blooming seasonal plants in the recipient's favorite colors

Gift Ideas for More Important Occasions

Potted plant

Larger planters with green and flowering plants

Bottle garden

Larger plants in hydropot

Elegant solitary plants

Indoor tree in an appropriate pot

Indoor fountain

Attractive Arrangements of Common Plants

In the winter months Cyclamen (*Cyclamen persicum*) is a fine choice for a flowering gift. You can buy it in a broad assortment of flower shapes and colors. In addition to the normal-size potted plants, you will find an increasing number of dwarf varieties. Here pink Cyclamen is combined with Persian Violet, Soleirolia, and Sword Fern.

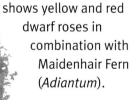

Miniatures for Every Occasion

People always appreciate a bouquet of flowers. An alternative that lasts a bit longer is flowering plants in miniature format. Depending on your budget, these make great gifts as individual plants or arrangements. There are no limits to the number of possible arrangements; the picture shows yellow and red dwarf roses in combination with Maidenhair Fern (*Adiantum*).

There are many beautiful arrangements among the wide variety of light-loving plants that make wonderful gifts.

Decorations for Advent and Christmas

Decorative plants are great for high-lighting the various seasons and major holidays such as Christmas, Easter, and Pentecost.

Here is a suggestion for a Christmas decoration using red and cream-colored Poinsettias (*Euphorbia pulcherrima*), which go beautifully with dark green evergreen branches. Combinations of Poinsettia in the same color but different sizes also look great in conjunction with shiny Christmas decorations.

Need Something Bigger?

A housewarming often calls for a fairly large gift; large solitary plants are a good choice, and they are always appreciated when people get their own house or move to a bigger apartment. You can't go wrong with easy-to-care-for plants for sunny to partially shaded locations. If you prefer to put several together, a small plant arrangement in appropriate cachepots is a good choice (here, Weeping Fig/*Ficus benjamina* with green and white variegated leaves, Fiddle Leaf Fig/*Ficus lyrata*, and Umbrella Tree/*Schefflera actinophylla*).

Hydroponics for Busy People

Many people would like to have some houseplants, but they don't have the time to take care of them properly, to water them, and feed them. In these cases, and for greening up office spaces, easy-to-care-for hydroponics plants as singles or arrangements are a good choice.

Here is a fairly large arrangement for a bright to partially shaded loca-tion consisting of Swiss Cheese Plant (*Monstera deliciosa*), Philodendron, and Silver Vine (*Epipremnum pinnatum*).

CROSS REFERENCE
Springtime greeting, page 145
Fall accents, page 145

CROSS REFERENCE
Easy care with hydroponics, pages 106–107

Adding Greenery to Shaded Places

Overview

Shade-Tolerant Climbing Plants

Philodendron, Ivy, Ivy Tree, Silver Vine, Creeping Fig, Climbing Philodendron, Grape Ivy, Syngonium, Kangaroo Vine

Shade-Tolerant Hanging Plants

Staghorn Fern, Spider Plant, Youth on Age, Strawberry Begonia, Tradescantia

Shade-Tolerant Shrubs

Parlor Palm, Leafy Begonia, Dieffenbachia, Peace Lily, Flamingo Flower, Clivia, Silver Spear, Maranta, Bird's Nest Fern, Schefflera, Cast Iron Plant, Bush Begonia, Alocasia, Calla Lily, Peperomia

Houseplants for a North Window

Plant that can get by on a little less light also have the advantage of being fairly easy to care for. In spite of their robustness, we should at least give the relevant plants a place near the window, if there's not enough room on the windowsill.

Among the plants that like shade and partial shade, there are a number of green plants with attractively colored leaves, such as the numerous varieties of leafy Begonias, plus some flowering plants such as Streptocarpus, Peace Lily, Flamingo Flower, Columnea, Lipstick Plant, Blooming Bush Begonias, and African Violet.

A warm north window is ideal for foliage and Bush Begonias, ferns, and bromeliads, and for lots of plants that come from the tropical rain forest, where they grow under the protective canopy of large trees and bushes.

The picture shows (from left to right) Peace Lily (*Spathiphyllum*), Spider Plant (*Chlorophytum comosum*, hanging), Ivy, Clivia, and Philodendron.

EXPERT ADVICE
In the winter, be sure that the window is well sealed.

Every home has places that are not well lighted, but that's no reason to forgo attractive greenery.

Light-Tolerant Climbing Plants

Silver Vine (*Epipremnum pinnatum*) and Ivy (*Hedera*) are unbeatable for their tolerance of light and water, and even the Heartleaf Philodendron (*Philodendron scandens*), with its easygoing nature and eagerness to grow, is an ideal plant for beginners. All three are perfectly suited for greening up a dark corner or for dividing a fairly large room. They can be combined with Parlor Palm, Philodendron, and *Dracaena marginata*.

Tropical Greenery

We can keep lush, high-growing plants even in rather dark rooms with such plants as Dragon Plant (*Dracaena marginata*), Swiss Cheese Plant (*Monstera deliciosa*), and one of the many Philodendron varieties. There are also variegated types of Swiss Cheese Plant and Philodendron that have multicolored leaves that don't look so massive but are a little more sensitive and dependent on light than the green-leafed strains.

Colors for Darker Locations

Annual and seasonal blooming plants, sometimes known as "throwaway plants" since often they can't be made to bloom a second time, are great for filling darker places with bright and luxuriant color. These include long-stem Azaleas, Primrose, Cyclamen, Clustered Bell Flower, and the shiny green of the tough leaves of Maidenhair fern (*Adiantum*), which also thrives as a solitary plant in partial shade.

EXPERT ADVICE
Types of Cissus respond well to cutting back.

CROSS REFERENCE
*Attractive tubs of color, pages 90–91;
Ephemeral blooming plants,
pages 92–93*

Display Windows for Every Taste

Overview

Fragrant Plants

Persian Violet, Scented Geranium, Fairy Primrose, Hyacinth, Jasmine, Stephanotis, Wax Plant

Spring Bloomers

Amaryllis, Cinerearia, Azalea, Wine Cup Primrose, Hyacinth, Clivia, Columnea, Crocus, Narcissus, Thanksgiving Cactus, Slipper Plant, Primrose, Parlor Maple, Tulips, Calla Lily

Summer Bloomers

Streptocarpus, Regal Pelargonium, Flamingo Flower, Barbeton Daisy, Zebra Plant, Hibiscus, Ixore, Chenille Plant, Urn Plant, Lipstick Plant, African Violet, Desert Rose

Fall and Winter Bloomers

Cyclamen, Chrysanthemum, Flamingo Flower, Passion Flower, Pentas, Poinsettia

An Herb Garden in the Kitchen Window

The windowsill in the kitchen is a great place to set up a planter with various kitchen herbs. It's a good idea to put individual herb pots in a large container so you have just one container to move aside when you open the window and can easily replace used-up herbs with new ones. The photo shows Common Thyme, Bush Basil, Lemon Grass, Tulbagia, and Society Garlic.

Good Scents

Many houseplants provide joy through other means than lively greenery and colored blooms; they also emit pleasant fragrances. The best-known and easiest-to-care-for representative of fragrant houseplants is the Scented Geranium, which smells like mint, rose, lemon, or nutmeg, depending on the variety. The arrangement includes (from left to right) Persian Violet (*Exacum affine*), *Pelargonium grandiflorum*, and *P. graveolens*.

A windowsill is the ideal place for arrangements involving many types of houseplants.

A Sunny Springtime Greeting

To drive winter away, various early spring bloomers are brought into the house; here, Yellow Narcissus and orange and lilac Crocuses in bright yellow pots.

Brilliant Colors and Strong Fragrance

Hyacinths provide more than just bright colors; they also bring intense fragrance into the house, and they make a perfect welcoming committee in halls and entryways.

The Joy of Summer Brought Indoors

In the summer, geraniums beautify terraces and decks, and Regal Pelargonium is a good choice for decorating living rooms. Several different colored varieties placed together bring all of summer's brightness into the house. Since there are many blooming plants available in the summer months, you can also arrange them according to various themes, such as Mediterranean (using Bougainvillea, Oleander, citrus trees, Lavender, Rosemary, and Sage) or tropical (with Hibiscus, Dipladenia, and Passion Flower).

Shades of Autumn

At this time, you can get lush blooming pot Chrysanthemums and Scottish Heather, which can be placed in the entryway or in a bright hallway. Blooming plants in warm yellows and reds can go near a window, in combination with other plants found wild.

In the picture (from left to right): Peperomia, red Flowering Begonia, Wax Plant (*Hoya*), dark Leafy Begonia, yellow Flowering Begonia, and Australian Ivy (*Muehlenbeckia adpressa*).

EXPERT ADVICE
For additional decoration, add some sprigs of hazel, willow, or broom.

EXPERT ADVICE
Fall accessories include nuts, rose hips, evergreen cones, and gourds.

Indoor Fountains and Bottle Gardens

Overview

Plants for Indoor Fountains

Philodendron, Peace Lily, Flamingo Flower, Dieffenbachia, Dragon Plant, Ivy, Silver Vine, Creeping Fig, Silver Spear, Croton, Syngonium, Schefflera, Umbrella Plant

Plants for Bottle Gardens

Miniature strains of Soleirolia, Dragon Plant, Ivy, Net Leaf, Maidenhair Fern, Artillery Plant, Creeping Fig, Croton, Creeping Moss, Bird's Nest Fern, Cretan Brake, African Violet, Peperomia

The Soothing Trickle of Water

This indoor fountain with copper plumbing has two things that people find soothing: the beneficial effect of green plants (Areca Palm, Syngonium, and variegated Ivy) and the soothing trickle of the water as it runs from one level to the next.

If the indoor fountain is large enough, it can also add to the humidity in the room and trap tiny particles in the air, such as house dust and smoke.

Indoor Fountains with Running Water

This indoor fountain has two water courses and Areca Palm, Dragon Plant, and Croton; it functions as a dual "circulatory system," since the water supply for the plants is separate from the fountain and the plants can be watered and fertilized according to their needs.

With dual systems like this, be sure that the water from the fountain always flows into the appropriate drain pot so that the fountain doesn't go dry.

EXPERT ADVICE
Use plants in hydroponics to green up indoor fountains.

EXPERT ADVICE
Use lime-free water for indoor fountains.

Indoor fountains with plants do more than look beautiful: they also increase the humidity in the room. Bottle gardens have their own microclimate.

A Miniature Greenhouse in a Bottle

A bottle garden makes a nice gift or an attractive focal point; it's a small and economical variation of a plant display case that can be installed in many different types of glass containers.

Here are a few bulbous and oblong glass containers planted with miniature strains of Creeping Moss (*Selaginella kraussiana*), Dragon Plant (*Dracaena*), Artillery Plant (*Pilea*), Net Leaf (*Fittonia verschaffeltii*), Croton (*Codiaeum variegatum*), and African Violet, and decorated with gravel and pieces of roots.

Making a Bottle Garden

First we use a paper funnel or tube to put some potting soil into the bottle. The layer of soil should be at least two inches (5 cm) deep. It would also be ideal to have another inch (2 cm) of gravel under the soil to collect excess water and keep the soil from becoming too moist.

Use a spoon tied to a stick to spread the soil evenly, and then use a thick piece of wood to prepare the holes for the plants.

Putting the Plants In

Carefully use a spoon and a fork with extensions tied onto them to lower the small plants into the prepared holes. Using a piece of wood or a cork secured to a stiff piece of wire, tamp the earth down well around the roots.

Watering

When all the plants are in place—the largest in the center—water them well. Be sure to keep the leaves from getting wet. Then close the bottle with a cork. If the inside fogs up too much, leave the vessel open for a few days.

EXPERT ADVICE
Only miniature strains are suited to bottle gardens.

EXPERT ADVICE
You can beautify the bottle garden by covering the soil with pebbles.

Suggestions for Amateur Gardeners

Overview

Poisonous Houseplants

Alocasia, Amaryllis, Primrose, Crown of Thorns, Dieffenbachia, Ivy, Chenille Plant, Clivia, Croton, Ponytail Palm, Oleander, King Sago Palm, Poinsettia, Desert Rose, Ornamental Pepper, Asparagus Fern

Thorny or Spiny Houseplants

Agave, Aloe, Crown of Thorns, Cactuses, Ponytail Palm, King Sago Palm, Yucca

Exotic Plants Grown from Seed

Avocado, Date Palm, Ginger, Mango, Orange Tree, Papaya, Passion Fruit, Citrus Trees

A Mini-Environment in a Terrarium

Here's what you need to set up a miniature environment in a terrarium: a glass terrarium that's not too large (an old aquarium will also work), gravel or vermiculite, potting soil, small plants, and pebbles, twigs, leaves, moss, or shredded bark for decoration.

First put in about an inch (3 cm) of gravel or clay pellets and cover it with about two to four inches of potting soil. Make some recesses for the plants with a spoon and then set the plants into place, with the largest ones at the edge and the smaller ones toward the center. Then tamp the soil down well and water carefully.

Now the planter can be decorated with roots or twigs, stones, leaves, moss, and shredded bark. A small porcelain frog or lizard will complete the miniature environment.

Many children are interested in nature and enjoy watching, growing, and propagating plants in the house and garden.

Growing Cress

Cress grows very quickly:

To germinate it needs only three to four days. It doesn't even need soil; it will even grow on damp paper, damp cotton, or clay figurines, as here with the cress hedgehog and the cress sun.

Place clay figurines into water at room temperature for a few hours until they are waterlogged. Then sow the cress seeds and cover the container with clear plastic wrap or a glass dish. As soon as the seeds germinate, take off the covering and keep the sprouts moist.

Colorful Hyacinth Sprouts

Here's how to proceed:

Fill special hyacinth glasses with tap water so that there is a quarter-inch (.5 cm) of space between the bottom of the bulb and the surface of the water. To encourage rooting, keep the glass in a cool (46–54°F/8–12°C), dark place for eight to ten weeks, adding water as needed. Once there are lots of white roots and the bud sticks out of the bulb about two inches (5 cm), the glasses have to be put into a warm place with a cover over the bud. Take off the cover when the flower bud begins to push it upward.

Growing Exotic Plants from Scratch

You can grow a plant from the seed of a ripe avocado fairly easily:

Wash off the seed, let it dry well, skin it, and stick it broad end down about an inch (2–3 cm) in slightly moist potting soil. Cover with clear plastic wrap or an overturned glass (use sticks to keep plastic wrap away from seed and tie it off around the pot); keep it in a warm, bright place. Keep protected from sun and spray it to keep it slightly damp. As soon as the first leaves appear, take the wrap off for a couple of hours every day. Then remove the wrap and set the plant in a warm, bright place.

EXPERT ADVICE
Beans and sunflowers also sprout very quickly.

CROSS REFERENCE
Plant propagation, pages 64–67

Technical Terminology

There are quite a number of technical terms that apply to growing houseplants. They may be new to some people, so here are some brief explanations.

Biological Pest Control: Combating pests without using chemicals, i.e., with living organisms.

Bromeliads: Pineapple-type plants with rosette-type leaf growth.

Chlorosis: Yellow coloring in leaves caused by lack of iron.

Climbing Plants: Plants with long shoots that need a support or a trellis to climb upward.

Container plants: Large warm-weather plants, such as Bougainvillea, Oleander, and Parlor Maple, that can be placed on decks or terraces during the summer months, but must spend the winter in a frost-free area. Since most of them grow in large pots, the label *container plants* has stuck.

Epiphytes: Plants (e.g., Bromeliads, Orchids, and many ferns) that grow on trees, whose branches and stems merely serve as a substrate. Nutrients are simply taken from rainwater.

Eye: A bud on a stem from which a new shoot grows.

Fertilizer sticks/stakes: Special commercial form of long-acting fertilizer.

Flypaper: Sticky bug catcher made of glue-coated paper or card stock that attracts certain insects by scent or color.

Gray Mold: A fungal infestation that covers plant parts with a gray-brown mold.

Ground Cover: Plants that spread out as they grow (e.g., *Ficus pumila*) and provide good ground cover.

Humidity: Quantity of water in the air. Warm rooms can hold a lot more humidity than cool ones.

Hydroponics: Growing plants in water and nutrients provided by special containers, rather than in soil. Watering and feeding are needed less frequently than with soil culture.

Immersion: Method of watering plants gently. The pot is placed into water for up to three hours; afterward, the excess water is allowed to run off.

Legginess: Abnormal, spindly growth in plants caused by insufficient light and excessively warm temperatures, or by light only on one side of plant. Identifiable by light-colored, soft leaves and long stems.

Layering: Propagation process by which a lateral stem from a mother plant is covered with earth and trained upward. The stem grows roots at the site of the bend.

Long-Acting Fertilizer: Plant foods that give off the nutrients that plants need by releasing them into the soil gradually. The soil has to be sufficiently moist, or the nutrients can't be released. That's why it's important to keep the fertilizer sticks or stakes moist.

Mother Plant: A plant from which cuttings, plantlets, offsets, or runners are taken for the sake of propagation.

Offset: An offspring plant that forms on the mother plant, frequently in the case of plants whose leaves grow in a rosette pattern (e.g., Agave, Clivia, and Sansevieria).

Organic Fertilizers: Fertilizers that comprise organic substances, such as guano and ground horn.

Partial Leaf Cutting: Propagation using only a piece of a leaf.

pH: Measure of soil acidity; pH values greater than 7 designate a basic soil (usually containing lime); values less than 7 indicate acidic soil; a pH of 7 is regarded as neutral.

Photosynthesis: Chemical process by which plants use water, carbon dioxide from the air, and energy from the sun to make sugars.

Plantlets: Young plants that often already have roots and that are on the mother plant, as with Devil's Backbone (*Kalanchoë daigremontiana*).

Potting Soil: Commercially produced, high-quality growing soil for flowers that is suitable as substrate for most houseplants.

Powdery Mildew: A fungal infection that causes white, floury spots on flowers and leaves.

Runner: Long lateral shoot that gives rise to young plants already equipped with roots, or that form roots upon contact with the soil.

Solitary Plant: Large, attractive houseplant that deserves its own place in the home, since it thrives and looks best all by itself.

Stolon: Long lateral shoots that form new plants; either they already have roots, or form roots upon contact with soil.

Succulents: Plants with fleshy, juicy leaves that are capable of storing water (e.g., Christmas Cactus).

Thumb Test: A practical way of measuring the moistness of the root ball: use your thumb or forefinger to feel the dampness of the compost near the top of the root ball; if it's dry, the plant needs water. If the top of the soil feels moist, no watering is needed.

Top Cutting: The top three to four inches (8–10 cm) of a shoot that is cut off and used for propagation.

Transpiration: Loss of water through a plant's leaf pores.

Variegation: Pertaining to strains of green plants with white or yellow spotted or striped leaves.

Waterlogging: Situation where roots become saturated and plants wilt because the roots die from lack of oxygen.

Whole Leaf Propagation: Using a single leaf for plant propagation.

Winter Rest: Plants that are indigenous to northern latitudes need a rest in the cold, frosty, and dark months, during which they drop their leaves and largely interrupt their metabolism.

Helpful Magazines and Books

Magazines

Country Living Gardener. Hearst Communications, 959 Eighth Ave., New York, New York 10019

Garden Gate. 2200 Grand Ave., Des Moines, Iowa 50312; www.GardenGateMagazine.com

Horticulture, Gardening at Its Best. Subscription Service, P.O. Box 53880, Boulder, Colorado 80322-3880

Kitchen Gardener. Taunton Press, Inc., 63 South Main St., P.O. Box 5506, Newtown, Connecticut 06470-5506; www.kitchengarden.com

For Further Reading

Baker, Jerry. *Happy, Healthy Houseplants.* NAL, 1999

Biggs, Matthew. *Practical Guide to Growing Healthy Houseplants.* Whitecap Books, 1997

Chiusoli, Alessandro, and Boriani, Maria L. *Simon and Schuster's Guide to Houseplants.* (Nature Guide Series; illustrated). S&S Trade, 1997

Courtier, Jane, et al. *Indoor Plants: The Essential Guide to Choosing and Caring for Houseplants.* Penguin Putnam, 1997

Evans, John. *The Complete Book of Houseplants.* Viking Studio Books, 1994

Heitz, Halina. *Indoor Plants.* Barron's, 1994

Hessayon, Dr. D. G. *The House Plant Expert.* Sterling, 1999

Herwig, Rob. *Growing Beautiful Houseplants: An Illustrated Guide to the Selection and Care of More Than 100 Varieties.* Facts on File, 1992

Hodgson, Larry, et al. *Ortho's Complete Guide to Successful Houseplants.* Meredith Books, 1992

Kramer, Jack. *Easy Care Guide to Houseplants.* Creative Homeowner, 1999

Lammers, Susan. *All About Houseplants.* Meredith Books, 1992

McCollum, Susan, and Riley, Teena. *Plant Basics: A Manual for the Care of Indoor Plants.* McCollum Riley, 1994

Stuckey, Maggie. *The Houseplant Encyclopedia (Illus.).* Berkley Publishing, 1995

Swithinbank, Anne. *Gardeners' World Book of Houseplants: An A–Z of the Top 100 Houseplants.* Parkwest Publications, 1996

Index

Pages designated with an asterisk contain a thorough description of the plant in question.
Page numbers in bold type indicate color photos and illustrations.

The Author

Anja Flehmig is a serious student of biology and houseplant gardening. She has had a year of formal training as editor in nature book publishing. She is the author of various practically oriented books on houseplants and gardening.

Photo Credits

The photos in this book are by Friedrich Strauss, with the exception of:
Busek: page 15, lower right
Eisenbeiss: pages 82 right, 83 right;
Henseler: pages 36 top, bottom, 37 top middle, 46 right, 47 left and middle, 48, 49;
Reihnard: pages 81 middle, 98 left;
Schaefer: pages 36 top center, 37 top, bottom center, 46 top left, 47 right;
Wothe: pages 14 top left, top right, 15 left, middle
Zunke: page 51 top

The Translator

Eric A. Bye, M.A., is a freelance translator who works in German, French, Spanish, and English in Vermont.

Thanks

The publisher and author thank Sonnhild Bischoff for the help with the text.

Copyright

All inquiries should be addressed to:
Barron's Educational Series, Inc.
250 Wireless Boulevard
Hauppauge, New York 11788
http://www.barronseduc.com

Library of Congress Catalog Card No. 2001037647

International Standard Book No. 0-7641-5412-5

Library of Congress Cataloging-in-Publication Data
Flehmig, Anja.
    [Zimmer Pflanzen für Einsteiger. English]
    Indoor plants for beginners : plant care basics, choosing houseplants, suggested plants for every location / Anja Flehmig.; with more than 290 color photographs by Friedrich Strauss; [English translation by Eric A. Bye].
        p. cm.
        Includes bibliographical references (p.).
    ISBN 0-7641-5412-5
    1. Houseplants. I. Title.
SB419 .F5413 2002
635.9′65—dc21
                        2001037647

Printed in Hong Kong

9 8 7 6 5 4 3 2

When you choose houseplants, you have to consider where you will put them, how much time you can devote to caring for them. Here are some types of houseplants that are beautiful but easy to care for.

Sunny Locations

Easy to Care For	A Little More Demanding
American Agave	Epiphyllum
Aloe	Coleus
Crown of Thorns	Date Palm
Regal Pelargonium	Common Fig
Elephant Foot	Opuntia Cactus
Flaming Katy	Tillandsia
Rosary Vine / String of Hearts	Coconut Palm
Living Stones	Urn Plant
Ponytail Palm	Light Green Kalanchoe
Sansevieria	Thanksgiving Cactus
Desert Rose / Adenium	Pentas
	Silver Torch Cactus
	Golden Barrel Cactus
	Yucca
	Ornamental Banana
	Ornamental Pepper
	Mediterranean Fan Palm

Key

- Blooming houseplants (perennial or annual)
- Perennial houseplants whose attraction is their leaves (ornamental foliage plants)
- Houseplants that make good hanging plants
- Trailing houseplants

Ten Golden

1. **You have to like your plants**
   Buy only plants that you really like.

2. **Water as needed**
   Your plant needs water only when the top of the root ball is dry.

3. **Light is better than shade**
   Most plants appreciate a bright window. Only certain plants can tolerate searing sun and dark corners, though.

4. **Resting period in the winter**
   Many of our green houseguests need a bright but cool location in the winter months.

5. **Don't forget the fertilizer**
   Houseplants need fresh plant food every two to four weeks in the spring and summer.

Shaded Locations

Easy to Care For	A Little More Demanding
Dragon Plant	Fatshedera / Ivy Tree
Spider Plant	Peace Lily / Spathiphyllum
Climbing Philodendron	Staghorn Fern
Cast-Iron Plant	Creeping Fig
Ivy	Bird's Nest Fern
	Fatsia / Japanese Aralia
	Cissus